0.99

COUNSELLING IN THE PASTORAL AND SPIRITUAL CONTEXT

To Bob
with best wishes
David Lyall

New College

· COUNSELLING IN CONTEXT ·

Series editors
Moira Walker and Michael Jacobs
University of Leicester

Counselling takes place in many different contexts: in voluntary
and statutory agencies; in individual private practice or in a con-
sortium; at work, in medical settings, in churches and in different
areas of education. While there may be much in common in basic
counselling methods (despite theoretical differences), each setting
gives rise to particular areas of concern, and often requires specialist
knowledge, both of the problems likely to be brought, but also of
the context in which the client is being seen. Even common counselling issues vary slightly from situation to situation in the way
they are applied and understood.

This series examines eleven such areas, and applies a similar
scheme to each, first looking at the history of the development of
counselling in that particular context; then at the context itself, and
how the counsellor fits into it. Central to each volume are chapters
on common issues related to the specific setting and questions that
may be peculiar to it but could be of interest and value to counsellors working elsewhere. Each book will provide useful information
for anyone considering counselling, or the provision of counselling
in a particular context. Relationships with others who work in the
same setting whether as counsellors, managers or administrators
are also examined; and each book concludes with the author's own
critique of counselling as it is currently practised in that context.

Current and forthcoming titles

Elsa Bell: *Counselling in Further and Higher Education*
Judith Brearley: *Counselling and Social Work*
Dilys Davies: *Counselling in Psychological Services*
Pat East: *Counselling in Medical Settings*
David Lyall: *Counselling in the Pastoral and Spiritual Context*
Michael Megranahan: *Counselling at Work*
Janet Perry: *Counselling for Women*
Gabrielle Syme: *Counselling in Independent Practice*
Nicholas Tyndall: *Counselling in the Voluntary Sector*
Brian Williams: *Counselling in the Penal System*

COUNSELLING IN THE PASTORAL AND SPIRITUAL CONTEXT

David Lyall

OPEN UNIVERSITY PRESS
Buckingham · Philadelphia

Open University Press
Celtic Court
22 Ballmoor
Buckingham
MK18 1XW

and
1900 Frost Road, Suite 101
Bristol, PA 19007, USA

First Published 1995

A catalogue record of this book is available from the British Library

ISBN 0 335 19162 2 (pb)

Library of Congress Cataloging-in-Publication Data
Lyall, David, 1936–
Counselling in the pastoral and spiritual context / David Lyall.
p.   cm. — (Counselling in context)
Includes bibliographical references and index.
ISBN 0–335–19162–2 (pb)
1. Pastoral counselling — Great Britain.   I. Title.   II. Series.
BV4012.2.L92   1994
253.5 — dc20   94–26387   CIP

Typeset by Graphicraft Typesetters Ltd, Hong Kong
Printed in Great Britain by St Edmundsbury Press Ltd,
Bury St Edmunds, Suffolk

Contents

Series editors' preface

There are few subjects that divide people into camps and force them into distinctive attitudes so rapidly as religion does. It is undeniably one of the strongest forces in world society, even if it takes many different forms. Religion truly evokes contrasting feelings: some want nothing to do with it, feel angry about its influence on society and individuals, and almost fear what to do with religious questions should they arise in the context of counselling. For others their religion provides them with the foundation of their sense of meaning. In some places and at some times in history religion has been responsible for the most appalling crimes and conflicts, and has held back progress. In other places and at other times it has been a profoundly motivating force in individual, social and political development as well as in artistic and even scientific achievement.

It helps, perhaps, to disentangle the spiritual from religion, and to see the essence of this book as looking at the spiritual and pastoral dimension, as indeed the title suggests. Such a separation can never be complete, and organized religion may well pose particular difficulties for some clients, as well as in their own attitudes for some counsellors. Certainly the link between psyche and soul is an obvious one, even if the distinction between soul and spirit may be one that needs further exploration. While there are clear philosophical issues about the reality of the spiritual 'outside' the human frame, there can be few except the most prejudiced who do not recognize the essential spiritual quality of much of life's experience 'within' the human frame: sometimes the sense of awe and profound wonder; sometimes the elation and joy of relationships with people and with the natural world; sometimes the darkness and despair which is also a familiar part of spirituality; and sometimes the struggle with existential issues about anxiety guilt and death.

These deeply personal matters (it is sometimes more difficult to talk about our religious beliefs than it is about sex or death) have exercised the pastoral skills of clergy of one faith or another throughout time. There have been very different ways of addressing them, some tending towards giving definitive answers and reassurance, others engaging with the doubts and mysteries, and preferring the enigmatic to the dogmatic. Britain is a multicultural society, with different faith systems that within the counselling relationship need to be fully accepted even if they cannot always be fully understood. It is historically the Christian and the Jewish communities that have been those that have most fostered counselling in the spiritual and pastoral context most obviously – playing, for example, an important role in the formation of the British Association for Counselling. Other organized faith have been less obviously keen to integrate counselling, although the links between Buddhism and some other Eastern traditions and counselling, and between humanistic ideas about spiritually and mainstream counselling have also been important, if less generally known about.

For many reasons, not least the significance of religions in cultural tradition on the one hand, and the spiritual experience and religious questions of clients and counsellors on the other, this book is an important addition to the *Counselling in Context* series.

Moira Walker
Michael Jacobs

Preface and acknowledgements

As a divinity student at Edinburgh University in the early 1960s, I recall browsing in the library stacks among the books on ministry and coming across a book I had not seen before. Apparently no one else had seen it either because some of the pages were still uncut. I began to read it. An hour later I was still reading. The book was Seward Hiltner's *Pastoral Counseling* (1949). It transformed my thinking about pastoral ministry because, with its case-histories and verbatims, it pointed to a new way of doing ministry, of being a pastor, of reflecting and writing about ministry.

Chance encounters such as these (if a Presbyterian can dare to dally with such an idea) give structure and content to the stories of our lives. In a sense, the past thirty years have been an attempt to work out the implications of the encounter with that book for my own ministry: first as a parish minister, then as a hospital chaplain and now in academic life.

The plot of my own story has been thickened by other chance encounters. A casual conversation at a conference late at night with Dr Ron Sunderland, then Director of the Institute of Religion at the Texas Medical Center, led to my spending three months in Houston where he introduced me to Clinical Pastoral Education, supervision and his own inspired approach to lay pastoral care. Although that was in 1976, writing this book has made me aware how much I owe to that experience.

My involvement in this book grew out of another casual conversation, this time with Michael Jacobs in the lunch queue at a meeting! I should like to acknowledge his skilled, supportive editing and the many helpful suggestions he made as each chapter was written.

My thanks are due to many other people especially to those who have allowed me to be their pastor, and to colleagues with whom I have been involved in ministry and from whom I have learned much. Among those who have been of direct help in the writing of this book I should especially like to thank the Reverend Brian Hilsley who drew upon his experience as a lawyer to research for me the legal aspects of confidentiality in the pastoral context, and Dr Derek Murray who read the manuscript and made many helpful suggestions about its style and content. My colleague, Dr Frank Whaling, was especially helpful in commenting on the draft of the section dealing with the pastoral relationship in the non-Christian religions. The bulk of the writing was done during study leave in the autumn term of 1993. Study leave for one member of a department means a heavier burden for others. I should like to thank Professor Duncan Forrester and my colleagues in the Department of Christian Ethics and Practical Theology at Edinburgh University not only for the extra work they undertook but also for the ongoing stimulation and encouragement which is so much a feature of working in the department.

Finally, I should like to thank Margaret, my wife and companion on the journey, for her constant love and support.

· ONE ·

The development of counselling in the pastoral and spiritual context

Counselling in a pastoral or spiritual context is characterized by complexity. Fifty years ago it might have been possible to confine our exploration to a study of the pastoral care offered by the or- dained ministers of the Christian Church (who were nearly all male). This is no longer possible. For one thing there is now much greater diversity of ministry within the Church, both lay and ordained, and many women and men regard themselves as offering a counselling ministry. For another, there are many people on the fringes of the Church, and even outside it, who would regard the counselling they do as having a pastoral or spiritual dimension.

Even within the Christian (or post-Christian) tradition of Britain in the 1990s there are very different understandings of the nature of counselling. On the one hand there are those who call them- selves pastoral counsellors heavily dependent upon the secular thera- pies; on the other, avowedly Christian counsellors base their approaches upon what they believe to be Biblical truth, and they are much more ambivalent towards the insights of psychology.

There are other considerations that introduce complexity into the study of counselling in a pastoral and spiritual context. In the rich diversity of our multicultural society, the different religious tradi- tions each have their own ways of providing personal support for people. Any comprehensive study of counselling in a pastoral and spiritual context must also take into account the contribution and insights of different cultural and ethnic groups.

Counselling in the pastoral or spiritual context has much in com- mon with counselling in other contexts. Yet even in the midst of today's pluralism there is a uniqueness to the counselling in this particular context which lies in its long history. Indeed, it has been argued that the roots of the modern counselling movement are themselves deeply embedded in the traditions of the Church's ministry of pastoral care. In *The Faith of the Counsellors* (1965) Halmos draws explicit parallels between Christian values and the professional values of the modern counsellor, of which he writes:

> there is always an unconfessed hope, a secret conviction even, that all the cultivating of little personal salvations, this gentle tending to circumscribed and limited anomalies, will somehow in the end add up to a comprehensive moral purpose, a kind of humanistic Kingdom of God.
>
> (Halmos 1965: 28)

Another writer who finds parallels between some of the key concepts of present-day pastoral counselling and some aspects of the thought and practice of the early Church is the American pastoral theologian, Tom Oden. Some quotations that appear in his book *Pastoral Counsel* (1989) illustrate this particularly well:

> (a) Show compassion for those who are bound in chains, as if you yourself were bound with them . . . Suffer with those who are in trouble, as if being in trouble with them.
>
> (Oden 1989: 8)

In this letter written by Ambrose, the fourth century Bishop of Milan, especially in the words 'as if', Oden sees an anticipation of what modern counsellors would understand as **empathy**.

> (b) Whatever experience comes your way, accept it as a blessing, in the certainty that nothing happens without God. Never equivocate, either in thought or speech . . . Do not be one of those who stretch out their hands to take, but draw back when the time comes for giving.
>
> (Oden 1989: 15)

In this radical openness to experience which we find in this second century *Epistle of Barnabas*, Oden sees prefigured the **congruence** deemed to be required of a good counsellor.

> (c) When people see that you unfeignedly love them, they will hear anything or bear anything from you . . . We ourselves will take all things from one that we know entirely loves us.
>
> (Oden 1989: 29)

Moving forward a thousand years, Oden sees in the love extolled by Thomas Aquinas in this third reference an affirmation of the need for the **unconditional acceptance** without which no counselling relationship can be productive.

Oden also finds within the writings of the early fathers some anticipation of the insights of psychoanalysis. For example, in the fourth century, John Chrysostom in his *Homilies on Ephesians* has something to say about the adverse effects of the repression of anger.

> There are some, like those dogs that bite secretly, which do not bark at all at those that come near them, nor are angry, but fawn, and display a gentle respect; but when they catch us off our guard, will fix their teeth in us. These are more dangerous than those that take up open enmity . . . Dost thou not know that those conflagrations are the most destructive of all which are fed within not those that are without? . . . Nothing good, nothing beautiful, can ever come from a bitter soul; nothing but misfortunes, nothing but tears.
>
> (Oden 1989: 249)

And in Clementine literature of the third and fourth centuries, Oden finds an intriguing passage which suggests that present relationships recapitulate past relationships.

> In all things, the end for the most part looks back upon the beginning and the issue of all things is similar to their commencement.
>
> (Oden 1989: 254)

Whatever credence is given to Oden's research into the pastoral insights of the fathers of the church, and whether or not we believe that he is identifying concepts of unchanging relevance or simply reading back modern insights into ancient documents, he undoubtedly demonstrates that throughout its history, some kind of pastoral care has been integral to the very nature of Christian community.

Clebsch and Jaekle (1964) have identified four different modes of pastoral care – sustaining, reconciling, healing and guiding – and have demonstrated how each in turn has been dominant in different epochs of the history of the Church. The earliest Christians lived with the expectation that the world would suddenly come to an end, and at this time the main pastoral task was to sustain faithful Christians as they awaited the *parousia*. The years AD 180–AD 305 were characterized by oppression, and a critical issue for the Church was the reconciliation of those Christians who had worshipped the

Emperor. When, under Constantine, Christianity became the 'official' religion ('You are all Christians now'), **guiding** persons to live within the Christian culture assumed prominence. The monastic revival was a reaction to the inevitable diminution of Christian standards and the cure of souls found useful in the monastries, a kind of **inductive guidance**, also became the norm for pastoring ordinary people. In the Middle Ages, with its well-defined sacramental sys-, tem, **healing** became the dominant mode of pastoral care since the sacraments themselves were believed to have therapeutic power. At the Reformation, **reconcilation** again became a major theme with the concern of the individual to find him/herself righteous before God. The Enlightenment saw the emphasis shift towards the pastoral task of sustaining people to live a Christian life in an increasingly secular world. Finally, the modern era has been characterized by the **eductive guidance** of a pastoral care heavily influenced by the secular psychotherapies. Of course, in every era all four modes of pastoral care have been in operation and the dominant mode has been no more than that, reflecting the main needs of people at that particular time.

So far, I have only examined pastoral care in the Christian tradition, and of course other religious communities have their distinctive patterns of caring for people. I will turn to these in the next chapter. It is worth noting, however, that the Jewish community also has a long tradition of mutual care with great emphasis upon the importance of the family and a strong reciprocal relationship between home and religion. It is perhaps no coincidence that many psychotherapists have been Jewish (Cooper 1988). The most significant was Sigmund Freud who, though he described himself as a 'godless Jew', was passionately, even obsessively, interested in the religious quest of humankind.

Notwithstanding its long history, in order to understand the nature of counselling in the pastoral and spiritual context of the late twentieth century it is necessary to study developments from earlier in the twentieth century. Inevitably we must begin with the work of Sigmund Freud and the impact of his views both upon human growth and development and the nature of helping relationships.

THE INFLUENCE OF FREUD

Of the many different kinds of helping relationships, there are few, if any, which have remained immune from the ideas of Freud. His psychoanalytic understanding of the human personality has given us new ways of thinking about people, as well as having a profound influence on the work of all the caring professions. Halmos writes:

> It was only in this century, after the Freudian explorations began to be understood, that advice-giving by the reponsible and learned and even pious professional became suspect. From the psychoanalytical clinical explorations a new method of helping others in some personal or private predicament has developed, which prescribes that the person in need of help should be assisted to discover more about the history of his preferences and aversions, and that he should be assisted to make his decisions in the light of new insight, more or less spontaneously gained, and not in the light of directives or advice given.
>
> (Halmos 1965: 1)

Conventional religion has not always seen itself as having an ally in Freud, which is not surprising in the light of his openly expressed antireligious philosophy. In *The Future of an Illusion* (1927a) he portrayed religious ideas as the product of man's attempt to come to terms with his own sense of helplessness in a hostile world, ideas generated by memories of the helplessness of his own childhood and, at a deeper level, of the childhood of the human race. These views were never going to endear him to the religiously orthodox. Nevertheless the theories of Freud and of those who came after him did come to exercise a profound influence on pastoral ministry. Understandably, pastoral ministry could not remain in isolation from the new understandings of people and relationships which were transforming other older professions like medicine and creating new ones such as social work. But perhaps more significantly there were a number of ministers who saw that they did not have to accept Freud's philosophical and metapsychological assumptions in order to benefit from his insights into the working of the human psyche.

Oskar Pfister

One of the first ministers to adopt Freudian ideas was the Swiss pastor, Oskar Pfister, with whom Freud engaged in a lengthy and mutually appreciative correspondence from 1909 to 1937 (Freud and Pfister 1963). In an editorial introduction to this volume of letters, the editor, Heinrich Meng, writes:

> During the first years of his ministry, Pfister wrote a paper protesting against 'the sin of omission towards psychology of present day theology'. In 1908 he came across the work of

Freud which provided him with the tool for which he had long sought, enabling him to give additional aid to those for whom his spiritual aid alone had been insufficient.

(Freud and Pfister 1963: 8)

Over the years Pfister incorporated many of Freud's psychoanalytic insights into his own pastoral practice and, according to Mein, had considerable influence upon Freud himself. Why did Freud, the atheistic Jew, give so much support to the Swiss pastor? Perhaps part of the answer lies in Freud's conviction that psychoanalysis should not remain wholly within the medical profession. In his *Postcript to the 'Question of Lay Analysis'* he writes:

My thesis was that the important question was not whether an analyst had a medical education but whether he has had the special training necessary for the practice of analysis.

(Freud 1927b: 252)

According to his first major biographer, Ernest Jones (1964: 580–6), Freud believed that while psychoanalysis could be practised by properly trained lay (i.e. non-medical) people, lay analysts should not work independently of the medical profession since, not being able to make a medical diagnosis, they were not competent to decide which patients were suitable for analysis. With this proviso, Freud believed that lay people could function as analysts as effectively as doctors and sometimes more effectively because a medical education could render a doctor unfit to practise psychoanalysis! Yet Freud never lost his reservations about ministers. In a letter to Pfister, written in 1927, he almost implies that Pfister was too nice to be a psychoanalyst. Recalling Pfister as he had known him fifteen years before, Freud writes to Pfister:

I pictured you in my mind as you were then, with all your winning characteristics, your enthusiasm, your exuberant gratitude, your courageous integrity, the way you blossomed forth after your first contact with analysis, as well as your blessed confidence in people who were soon to disappoint you . . . I could not help feeling regret that the battle had passed you by.

(Freud and Pfister 1963: 108)

Despite this ambivalence on Freud's part, there was such a core of deep mutual respect that in 1934 Freud could write to his friend:

That you should be a convinced analyst and at the same time a clerical gentleman is one of the contradictions which make life interesting.

(Freud and Pfister 1963: 142)

Three British minister-therapists

The contributions of three British clergy might lead to a similar judgement to Freud's on Pfister. J. G. McKenzie, a congregationalist teaching at Paton College, Nottingham, was one of the first ministers to be aware of the implications of Freud's work for the practice of ministry. His initial concern was with theological education and he began *Souls in the Making: An Introduction to Pastoral Psychology* (1928) with a chapter boldly headed 'What Ministerial Education Lacked'. This lack was any systematic attempt to relate the study of academic theology to the practical work of the ministry. McKenzie goes on to give a provisional answer to his search for a way of integrating theology and practice:

> I turned then to the study of 'The New Psychology' for which I had a fair preparation. Fortunately I had kept up my studies in philosophy, ethics and academic psychology . . . My interest was not speculative; it was eminently practical; it arose out of the needs of pastoral work and preaching. I wanted to understand the processes behind behaviour; whether it was possible to direct the mind towards interests that make for character; whether it was possible to understand how differences in character, temperament and personality arose; how temptations came and how they are overcome. After an extensive study of the psychoanalytic view, I was convinced that it had much to teach the teacher, preacher and educationalist generally.
>
> (McKenzie 1928: 3)

McKenzie tells how further experiences of pastoral work convinced him that the new psychology was indeed an effective tool for coping with the myriad of human problems encountered in any busy pastorate. The remainder of the book is an attempt to relate the Freudian understanding of personality to the practice of ministry. McKenzie spent a lifetime teaching, practising clinical psychotherapy and writing; his last book (on guilt) was published in 1962.

A second British minister who made a critical analysis of the contribution of modern psychological theories to pastoral work was the methodist Leslie D. Weatherhead. His *Psychology, Religion and Healing* (1951) was a critical study of all non-physical methods of healing, in which *inter alia* he considered the contribution of Freud, Jung and Adler to the cure of souls. His opinion was that while Freud had made a distinctive contribution to the understanding of mental illness, nevertheless:

> after analysis there must be synthesis and in the latter . . . religion can play a vital part. I feel that the fundamental weakness of

Freudian psychoanalysis is the entire lack of interest in a subsequent re-orientation or synthesis.
                                    (Weatherhead 1951: 251)

While this judgement might not be accepted by some, or might
be expressed in different terms by others, Weatherhead did recognize the need for pastors to take cognizance of the new psychologies
for a proper understanding of the person. Further, he was a prolific
and popular author, and his many books directed at church con-
stituencies helped to create a more favourable environment for an
approach to pastoral care that took Freud seriously.

Mention must also be made of a third minister-psychotherapist,
not only because of the importance of his own work, but also
because of his influence upon a doctor who was to make a critical
contribution to the development of pastoral counselling in Britain.
Harry Guntrip, like McKenzie, was a congregationalist minister who
found a complementary vocation in psychotherapy and in working
out the relationship between his two callings. In turn he was to
make a profound impact upon Frank Lake, the founder of Clinical
Theology, whose ideas will be examined below. Guntrip himself
was greatly influenced by W. R. D. Fairbairn, an Edinburgh psychoanalyst, active in the period 1930–1950, who went beyond Freud's
emphasis on the importance of the instincts in personality development to what has come to be known as Object-Relations Theory.
Fairbairn, along with Melanie Klein, saw limitations in Freud's
somewhat mechanistic understanding of instinctual and biological
drives. In simple terms Object-Relations theory pointed to the formation of the personality within the matrix of human *relationships*,
especially between mother and child. Looking back from our present
perspective in which our views on human growth and development
have been shaped by writers such as Klein and Winnicott, such
ideas may not seem very radical. Yet at the time they were a direct
challenge to Freud's theories and took time to be assimilated. Guntrip
became convinced that a practical understanding of psychotherapy
itself required a 'personal' rather than a 'biological' theory (1956).
Object-relations theory presented an understanding of the person
which was essentially more optimistic than the purely Freudian
theory based on instinctive drives. Two object-relations theorists
write

Guntrip believes the conclusions Freud's theory produces regarding human possibilities too grim. He considers drive theory
degrading to mankind and, on that basis, unacceptable.
                                    (Greenberg and Mitchell 1983: 213)

Biological instincts were 'given' and could only be either grati-
fied, repressed or sublimated. But if emotions were generated within
the matrix of human relationships then those aspects of the personality which had been formed in one relationship could be re-formed
in another. Thus in the psychotherapeutic relationship there was
hope because there was the possibility of transformation.

Like McKenzie, Guntrip too was convinced there was a serious
lack in theological education. In his *Psychology for Ministers and Social
Workers* (1971: 58), which ran to three editions between 1949 and
1971, he argued that in ministerial training, there should be something corresponding to the clinical training of medical students. He
was convinced that ordinands should not be left to their own un-
aided enthusiasm to acquire an adequate knowledge of psychology
and its bearing upon pastoral work. Much of the book is an attempt
to work out the implications of analytical psychology for the daily
work of ministers and social workers. Preaching, the leadership of
groups, home visiting and the care of anxious people are all set
within the theoretical framework of a personalist understanding of
analytical psychology.

Carl Gustav Jung (1875–1961)

An examination of the psychoanalytic influence on pastoral counselling would not be complete without reference to the work of one
of Freud's early disciples who later broke with him to form his own
theoretical base. The son of a Swiss pastor of uncertain faith, Jung
studied medicine and later pyschiatry at Basle. He became convinced of the validity of many of Freud's views and visited him in
Vienna, where on one occasion they apparently talked non-stop for
thirteen hours. For a time Jung was seen by Freud as his successor
but Jung could not accept some of Freud's central ideas and they
went their separate ways. Jung could not accept Freud's reductionism, his belief that all human behaviour could be explained in terms
of instinctive drives, nor his insistence that the roots of all pathology
were sexual. Similarly, Freud was troubled by Jung's positive evaluation of the place of religion in human life.

Jung's basic sympathy towards a religious world view has made
his theories of personality more acceptable to some Christians. In a
notable television interview towards the end of his life, Jung was
asked if he believed in God. After a long pause he said 'I do not need
to believe in God – I know.' Many Jungian analysts have a deep
interest in theology. There are, however, those who have found it
hard to accept the theological implications of Jung's religious ideas.

Jung's religion tends to be a mystic, esoteric, almost gnostic pheno-menon. He has problems with a Trinitarian God, finding in the 'quaternity' (foursome) a more complete symbol than one based on the number three. He therefore proposed two principal candidates for the fourth member of the Godhead, either 'evil' or 'the feminine'. These views are no more likely to endear him to the theologically orthodox than did Freud's atheism.

Nevertheless, some of Jung's understanding of how the mind works has become important in contemporary pastoral counselling. His main contribution to the working of the conscious mind lies in his theory of psychological types. Work based on the polarities of Extroversion-Introversion, Sensing-Intuition and Thinking-Feeling has been developed into the Myers-Briggs Type Indicator (MBTI) which is now widely used as a diagnostic tool in a variety of settings ranging from career guidance and team-building to spiritual direc-tion (Oswald and Kroeger 1988). But it has been Jung's insights into the functioning of the unconscious mind which have been of particular significance for pastoral counselling. He believes that the unconscious consists of two components, the personal unconscious and the collective unconscious, and it is the unconscious which provided the necessary resources for moving towards wholeness, a process he calls 'individuation'. Jung also believes that spiritual growth is a central indispensable dimension of all movement to-wards wholeness:

> However far-fetched it may sound, experience shows that many neuroses are caused by the fact that people blind themselves to their own religious promptings . . . The psychologist today ought to realise that we are no longer dealing with questions of dogma and creed. The religious attitude is an element in psychic life whose importance can hardly be over-rated.
>
> (Jung 1933: 67)

For Jung, the task of individuation, this harmonious integration of all aspects of one's personality, both positive and negative, be-longs to the second half of life:

> Among all my patients in the second half of life – that is to say, over thirty-five – there has not been one whose problem in the last resort was not that of finding a religious outlook on life.
>
> (Jung 1933: 229)

Two authors have been particularly helpful in integrating the Jungian insights into a Christian perspective. In Britain, the late

Christopher Bryant showed in *Jung and the Christian Way* (1983) how the process of individuation is fully compatible with the traditional Christian practices of self-examination, prayer and meditation and contemplation. The American episcopalian priest, Morton Kelsey, in his *Christo-Psychology* (1982) also develops a Christian psychology based on an integration of Jungian insights with classical Christianity. The contribution of Jung to pastoral ministry is promoted in Britain through the work of the Guild of Pastoral Psychology.

THE AMERICAN CONNECTION

No contemporary understanding of pastoral counselling in Britain and elsewhere is possible without an appreciation of the immense contribution made by individuals and movements in the United States over the past seventy years. This contribution, at least in its formative stages, was quite different in its theoretical orientation from that made by the Europeans. Pfister, McKenzie and Guntrip all sought to integrate psychoanalytic insights into the pastoral ministry of the Church. This was not the case in North America. In the early decades of the twentieth century, the dominant cultural influences on new approaches to pastoral care were the pragmatism and functionalism of the psychologist William James and the instrumentalism of the educationalist John Dewey. This new approach to pastoral care and counselling gave birth to an extensive literature with an international readership. In turn, this led people from many countries to seek training in America.

A pivotal figure in the development of pastoral counselling in the United States was Seward Hiltner, who taught pastoral care and counselling first at Chicago and then at Princeton Theological Seminary. Further, when there was very little literature on the subject elsewhere, his writing and that of other Americans filled the gap with the inevitable importation of American approaches into other countries. Among these authors might be included Carrol Wise (1951), Waynes Oates (1962) and later Howard Clinebell (1966).

Within the development of pastoral care and counselling in the United States it is possible to identify two quite distinct strands. The first lies in the development of Clinical Pastoral Education, the second in the growth of pastoral counselling as an autonomous professional discipline drawing on (at least initially) insights which stemmed from the work of Carl Rogers. These two movements were inevitably interrelated but they should not be confused with one another.

Clinical Pastoral Education

In 1925, the Reverend Anton T. Boisen, then Chaplain at Worcester State Hospital, Massachusetts, invited a small group of theological students to work with him in the hospital during the long summer vacation. At the time he was recovering from a psychotic break-down and that experience also brought home to him the current inadequacies in ministerial education. He was distressed that students for the ministry could still:

> pass through almost any of our theological schools . . . without ever having studied the human personality in health or disease (even though) the human personality was that through which it was the pastor's task to work.
>
> (Powell 1975: 9)

He therefore instituted his own programme at Worcester in the belief that there was no better laboratory for the study of people in crisis than the mental hospital and no better library than 'living human documents', a phrase that has become a watchword in this movement (Powell 1975: 3, 24).

There were others besides Boisen who saw the possibility of new directions in theological education based on the hospital. Richard C. Cabot, a Boston physician, had earlier developed a 'case-method' of teaching medical students and proposed a similar method to the teaching of theological students. In 1926 he published a paper in which he argued that divinity students, like medical students, should see their teachers grapple with difficult cases with varying degrees of success and failure. While Cabot was almost irrationally opposed to psychiatry, believing that most mental illness was of organic origin, he did give some financial backing to Boisen in his new approach to theological education. This support did not last: after a second breakdown, Boisen began to develop an understanding of mental illness whose origins were more social and psychological. In 1932, Boisen was appointed Chaplain at Elgin State Hospital in Chicago. This became a second locus for the development of clinical training, but with a quite different emphasis from the New England school. The years that followed were marked by bitter controversy between the two rival approaches to clinical training. One school of thought, characteristic of chaplains in psychiatric hospitals, empha-sized the need for students to gain insight and self-understanding and became institutionalized in the Council for the Training of Theo-logical Students. The other group, consisting mainly of chaplains in general hospitals, emphasized the acquisition of pastoral skills and techniques and formed themselves into the Institute of Pastoral Care based in New England. The story of the interrelationship of these two organizations is long and complicated and need not be examined in detail here. It was obvious that these differing emphases were not mutually exclusive, and after a prolonged courtship they, together with two smaller denominational organizations, joined together in 1967 to form the Association for Clinical Pastoral Education (Thornton 1970; Hall 1992).

Since the days of Boisen and Cabot a network of over three hundred centres has been developed in North America, mainly in hospitals and prisons, offering CPE courses. Some features are common to all of these courses which are structured in three-month segments or 'quarters' and open to students, pastors and lay people. There is the exercise of a meaningful pastoral ministry in the hospital or prison, reporting back to a qualified supervisor on these experiences of ministry, and interpersonal groups facilitating a process of personal and professional growth. Central to the whole process is the quality of supervision offered; this is generally of a high order with strict standards for the accreditation of supervisors. Many theological students benefit from a basic 'quarter' of CPE and many seminaries require this for graduation. Full-time hospital chaplains in the USA are normally required to have a year of this kind of training and an accredited chaplain-supervisor two further years.

This movement has had an important influence on the development of pastoral ministry internationally as well as in North America. There is, however, a second strand within the fabric of pastoral counselling on that continent.

Carl Rogers and Client-Centered Therapy

In his definitive history of pastoral care in America, Brooks Holifield (1983: 259) notes that after the Second World War, pastoral counsellors began to speak a new language. While most American ministers probably continued to exhort and instruct in their pastoral ministry as in their preaching, among pastoral theologians in the mainline theological schools – the new theoreticians of the cure of souls – exhortation and advice were out of fashion and 'self-realization' had become the in-word. Holifield lays this influence at the door of the American psychologist Carl Rogers and few would challenge this judgement. Over the past fifty years Rogers has continued to have an impact on virtually every area of counselling.

Born of fundamentalist parents in Illinois in 1902, Rogers seemed destined for the Protestant ministry and enrolled in New York's Union Theological Seminary. After a mind-broadening trip to China with the World Student Christian Federation, he rebelled against the narrowness of his upbringing and crossed the road to Columbia Teachers College where he was influenced by the educational theories of John Dewey with their emphasis on personal growth. For a number of years he worked as a child psychologist and began to develop the ideas which transformed our understanding of the process of counselling.

A succession of important books reflects the development of these ideas. His first major book *Counseling and Psychotherapy* (1942) introduced the concept of **non-directive counselling**, with his insistence that the counsellor should not interfere in the process of therapy but facilitate the self-expression and insight of the client by giving the client space to move forward autonomously. Advice-giving, confrontation or interpretretions by the counsellor are not allowed. If this was a prescription for what the counsellor must *not* do, Rogers' next book, *Client-Centered Therapy* (1951) emphasized the positive aspects of the counsellor's role, in particular the need for the counsellor to trust the client's capacity to change. In a third important book, *On Becoming a Person* (1961), Rogers expanded his thinking from the therapeutic relationship to all human relationships, the qualities of the former becoming the paradigm for such relationships as that between parent and child and teacher and pupil.

There emerged from Rogers' writings certain characteristics of the ideal helping relationship which have almost become normative for all types of counselling (and we have already noted how Tom Oden has tried to find examples of them in the pastoral ministries of the early Church). Enunciated by Rogers, they were thoroughly researched by Truax and Carkuff (1967) and described variously as (a) **genuineness, authenticity** or **congruence** by which is meant that the counsellor is consistent, self-aware and aware of his or her own limitations with a degree of openness in personal relationships; (b) **unconditional positive regard** or **non-possessive warmth** indicating that for counselling to be effective some degree of warmth must be communicated, the client being accepted without condemnation or labelling; and (c) **accurate empathy**, the ability to identify with and experience another's experience *and* the ability to communicate to the counsellee that this is so.

The aims of this approach to counselling are several: catharsis or the release of emotion, the achievement of a degree of insight setting the client free to change, an emphasis on the authority of the client's own experience and a belief in the possibility of personal growth. Implicit in these aims were the assumptions of mid-twentieth century America – an optimistic belief that all things are possible, which runs in the face of the determinism of both the Freudians and the behaviourists. It could be described as a 'plaster-cast' understanding of the therapeutic relationship. Just as when a broken limb is set in plaster the natural healing processes of the body take over until recovery is complete, so also an effective counselling relationship is one that provides a supportive environment in which the natural healing processes from within the human psyche restore health to deeply troubled people.

Rogerian methods of counselling began to be incorporated in the Pastoral Care courses in the seminaries. Brooks Holifield (1983: 303) writes:

> Rogers offered a method of counseling which could be taught – or at least introduced – in the brief period available in the seminary curriculum. One pastoral theologian who observed Rogers' 'determining influence' on pastoral counseling remarked that he offered 'a relatively safe method for a counselor of limited training'. The Rogerian method could prevent a minister from doing any harm. But Rogers was popular with the religious liberals because they liked his optimistic image of the self as capable of growth and change.
>
> (Holifield 1983: 303)

Holifield also shows that Rogers' ideas were not always universally accepted. Of particular fascination is an account of a dialogue in 1965 between Rogers and Paul Tillich on what turned out to be Tillich's last public appearance:

> it was not surprising that they could find much on which they could agree. But on a few questions they politely clashed. Rogers claimed that the capacities for self-actualization in a person were so powerful that the counselor needed only to create a sphere of freedom in which they could unfold. Tillich maintained that human nature is far more ambiguous than Rogers suggested and that the ambiguity would make it exceedingly difficult, if not impossible, for any counselor to create such a sphere of freedom. Rogers believed that 'estrangement' was imposed by cultural institutions. Tillich was convinced that it was a tragic and inevitable component in any process of maturation. Rogers argued that for the modern world, God was dead, and he wondered why Tillich continued to use a religious

vocabulary. Tillich insisted that scientific language is always limited in scope and that only the language of religious symbol and myth could point beyond itself to the unconditional Ground of all existence. Both men agreed about the importance of self-affirmation and acceptance, but Tillich added that the acceptance experienced in a human relationship was a prelude to an awareness of being accepted within 'the dimension of the Ultimate'.

(Holifield 1983: 332)

Interestingly, towards the end of his own life Rogers, the guru of humanistic psychology, would probably have shared more of Tillich's views. His last book, *A Way of Being* (1980) was much more aware of the transcendent and mystical dimension of human life.

Many ministers in the USA trained to be pastoral counsellors and exercised their new skills as part of their on-going ministry within the Church. Others, however, chafing under the restrictions of ecclesiastical institutionalism, found in these new skills the possibility of finding employment outside the parish in either Church-related or independent counselling centres. In a perceptive paper analysing this trend, James Dittes of Yale Divinity School wrote:

Personal counseling is resorted to by many theological students and ministers because it seems to offer a sense of purpose, relevance and achievement which they crave for in their ministry. The relevance is, in most instances, illusory and false: personal counseling is not nearly so effective as it frequently appears to the counselor to be and, when it is, its achievements cannot automatically be identified with the aims of Christian ministry. The fact that in spite of this so many men have turned so eagerly and so unquestioningly to counseling gives evidence of the powerful, even desperate, desires for 'relevance' which lies behind this particular post-war rush.

(Dittes 1961: 144)

Despite Dittes' strictures, in 1963 the American Association of Pastoral Counselors (AAPC) was formed, an organization initially designed for specialists in counselling and not for ordinary parish ministers. Most of its members were associated with pastoral counselling centres, of which there were then about one hundred and fifty, though some of the founders also supported the idea of private practice. While attention has been given to the seminal contribution of Carl Rogers, it must not be thought that his was the only, or even the dominant, therapeutic resource for all pastoral counsellors. By the time AAPC came into being a whole spectrum of secular psychotherapies was being utilized e.g. psychoanalysis, Jungian approaches, Transactional Analysis, Gestalt Therapy and Reality Therapy to name only a few. This rich diversity of therapeutic method inevitably carried its own price tag: a loosening of connection with the traditional modes of Christian ministry and a consequent loss of theological centre. This probably had to happen at that time in order to affirm the integrity of the secular therapies. The question today is whether some new kind of integration is possible. I shall return to this in a later chapter.

In exploring the American contribution to the development of counselling within the context of the community of faith, I have focused on the origins of what are arguably the two main organizations in the field: the Association for Clinical Pastoral Education and the American Association of Pastoral Counselors. While these movements have undoubtedly been important in the USA, internationally there have also been significant knock-on effects. First, an enormous body of literature has been generated, and in the absence of indigenous literature in terms of either volume or quality (this was certainly true of Britain until the 1980s), the works of American authors became both normative and formative. There can be few seminary courses on Pastoral Care throughout the world for which Howard Clinebell's *Basic Types of Pastoral Counseling* (1966) has not been prescribed reading. Further ministers and students from around the globe, perhaps stimulated by this literature, went to America for further training. The First International Congress on Pastoral Care and Counselling was held in Edinburgh in 1979. A preparatory meeting was held in Edinburgh the previous year and the opening session was attended by Ed Thornton, then Editor of the (American) Journal of Pastoral Care. He asked each of the fifteen or so members of that international committee what it was in their own pilgrimage that had brought them to the point of being involved in planning the Congress. He later wrote (1979):

> In the accents of German, Dutch, Norwegian, Italian and Scots I heard repeated reference to having done CPE in the United States twenty-three years ago . . . thirteen years ago . . . a few years ago. 'It was very exciting . . . an awakening . . . a new style of aggressiveness . . . wanting to keep up . . . to share what was important to me with others.'
>
> (Thornton 1979: 146)

The American influence was certainly important, but there were some significant developments in other countries, including Britain. To these I now turn.

THE BRITISH EXPERIENCE

In 1960 pastoral counselling in Britain was (literally) a closed book; but in 1979 the First International Congress on Pastoral Care and Counselling was held in Edinburgh. This event could not have been mounted without there having been significant developments in the United Kingdom during the intervening two decades. In fact the 1960s and 1970s saw the birth and growth of a number of organizations and courses, not all of them directly concerned with counselling, but together creating the network that gave the development of pastoral counselling in Britain its distinctive ambience. That network consisted of (i) one or two organizations committed to interdisciplinary dialogue; (ii) those involved in the development of Pastoral Studies within the universities; (iii) some pioneering attempts within the churches to promote pastoral counselling; and (iv) a number of organizations founded with the quite specific aim of furthering the practice of pastoral counselling and/or the training of counsellors. This network coalesced into the Association for Pastoral Care and Counselling, formed in 1972. APCC was one of the existing organizations which was to help form the British Association for Counselling; the other two were the Association of Student Counsellors and the National Association for Young People's Counselling and Advisory Services.

The promotion of dialogue

Closer co-operation between doctors and clergy in the care of the sick had long been a pious hope on the part of members of both professions: a conference to discuss the issue had been held as long ago as 1910 in the Chapter House of St Paul's Cathedral. Fifty years later, such co-operation was still being advocated, but little satisfaction was expressed at what was actually happening on the ground. Against this background two organizations, one in Scotland, the other in England, came into being to pursue the matter more intentionally.

In 1959 the Scottish Pastoral Association was founded 'to promote an exchange of ideas and a basis of co-operation among all who regard themselves as exercising a pastoral function'. This brought together ministers, doctors, nurses and social workers in a series of national conferences and local branch meetings which explored issues such as the problems of a particular age group, issues relating to how the caring professions could work together or attitudes to death. While the SPA had a crucial role in the personal and professional development of many ministers (and members of other professions) it closed itself down in 1976. Having set up two commissions to examine its continuing role, it had the courage to recognize that this in itself was probably a symptom of having none. The situation moved on at speed as other organizations developed issues pioneered by the Association. In fact the Association was absorbed into the more recently formed Scottish Institute of Human Relations, set up when Dr J. D. Sutherland retired to Edinburgh after being Director of The Tavistock Institute in London. The SIHR became a centre for psychoanalytic psychotherapy and training in Scotland and the North of England. A subsequent development of significance for pastoral counselling was the setting up of the Guntrip Trust (under the auspices of the Institute). Named after the pioneer pastor/psychoanalyst, the fund helps ministers to use the resources of SIHR either for personal therapy or for training. The driving force behind this move was Murray Leishman, then Chaplain at the Royal Edinburgh Hospital (psychiatric) who had also undertaken the full psychoanalytic training.

While the lifespan of the SPA was short, there were at least two further developments of continuing significance. The first was in pastoral education itself. In 1962 a group of Edinburgh divinity students, frustrated at the general lack of pastoral relevance in their training, approached the SPA to see if the Association would mount a course during the Easter vacation. Their contact was James Blackie, the university chaplain and a founder of the SPA. The minutes of the Executive Committee indicate that plans drawn up by James Blackie were approved, provided (a) that it would be conducted under the auspices of the SPA and (b) that students of other Theological Colleges were invited to take part. The content of the programme now seems fairly basic but in 1962 it was heady stuff: it included lectures on 'The Art of Counselling and the Accepting Relationship' and 'The Minister's Awareness of Himself as a Pastoral Factor', a symposium on 'What is Illness?' and visits to units in the general and psychiatric hospitals. The conference became an annual event and thirty years later a week-long hospitals' conference continues to be an integral component of the Faculty of Divinity's basic course on ministry.

A second off-shoot from the SPA, this time of wider British significance, was the launching in 1960 of the journal *Contact*, later sub-titled 'The Interdisciplinary Journal of Pastoral Studies'. Very soon the Institute of Religion and Medicine (IRM), and the Clinical Theology Association, themselves both very new, became sponsoring organizations and, despite early publishing crises, the journal became sufficiently well-established to survive independently after the demise of the SPA. Later, three other organizations – the Irish Pastoral Association, the Westminster Pastoral Foundation and the Association for Pastoral Care and Counselling – joined in sponsorship of the journal. The miracle of *Contact* is that after producing over one hundred and thirteen issues, and having weathered financial storms which had sunk other publications, *Contact* sails on, catching the winds of the contemporary scene in British pastoral counselling and, as we shall see later, sometimes contriving to be at the centre of the squall.

In England, the **Institute of Religion and Medicine** was established as the result of a conference of doctors and clergymen held at Lambeth Palace in 1962. The Archbishop of Canterbury set up a working party to consider the practical questions involved in promoting co-operation between the medical profession and clergy and ministers of all denominations. The outcome was the establishment of an Institute devoted to the study and advancement of matters of mutual interest to clergy and doctors based on the organizational model of a network of local groups embracing all professions in the broad field of spiritual, mental and physical health.

Dr Kenneth Soddy, one of the pioneers of the Institute, pointed out in an early issue of *Contact* (1964: 31) that while the SPA seemed to be 'religion-centred', this would not necessarily be the orientation of the IRM. Nevertheless, while in theory doctors need no more have religious convictions than the clergy should be experts in biology, it was unlikely that groups would be formed of doctors and clergy intolerant of one another. The aim of the IRM was to improve communication between students and practitioners of the two professions through work in medical schools and theological colleges and at postgraduate level.

One particular IRM project did have an impact upon the development of pastoral counselling. In 1966 and 1968, the Institute organized two consultations on *Practical Training in Pastoral Care Ministry*. These were chaired by Dr Ian Ramsey, then Bishop of Durham. They brought together staff from theological colleges and universities, Directors of Post-Ordination Training, hospital chaplains and indeed virtually anyone in Britain with a contribution to make to the debate about pastoral education. The Institute was also a major participant in another set of conversations going on almost simultaneously. The Consultative Committee on Training for Ministry of the British Council of Churches had set up a working party with the remit of investigating the place of psychological and psychiatric insights (1) in the content of theological training in the light of the pastoral task of ministers today; (2) in relation to the traditional subjects of theological education; (3) in developing methods of theological training; and (4) in fostering the spiritual growth of self-understanding of ordinands. Ian Ramsey was also convener of this working party. Inevitably there was a considerable degree of overlap in the two groups and their reports were published together in one volume (British Council of Churches 1968) with recommendations for the promotion of a more psychologically aware approach to pastoral training at all levels of theological education.

The colleges and universities

Whether as a result of the BCC/IRM report or simply as a more general interest in counselling in the secular arena, the theological colleges began to appoint Directors of Pastoral Studies. In a *Contact* article, Wharton (1983) describes the transition in the previous decade from 'pastoralia' to 'pastoral studies'. This had been facilitated by the Report of yet another working party, this time set up by the Church of England and chaired by Anthony Dyson. The Report, *Education for Pastoral Ministry*, published in 1976, was not concerned with the development of counselling skills in themselves but provided a context in which such skills could be developed and used as part of an on-going ministry. It was expected that a priest, some two to three years after ordination, would have achieved certain educational goals in relation to knowledge, skills, exposure to life in society and the church, and supervised practical experience.

In the late 1960s British universities expanded rapidly following the publication of the Robbins Report and the growth of pastoral studies as a distinct discipline was part of that expansion. Certificate or diploma courses were set up in Manchester, Birmingham and Cardiff and in the four ancient Scottish Universities. Central to all these courses were supervised placements in churches, hospitals and social service agencies, though one suspects that the quality of supervision varied greatly, this having been developed more intentionally in the secular arena. The Birmingham course was a particularly strong one under the direction of Michael Wilson, James Mathers and Robert Lambourne. All three had been medically trained, yet the significant contribution of the Birmingham course was to warn against a developing 'medicalization' of pastoral care. As I show later, this became a critical issue in the unfolding discussion about the nature of the pastoral counselling that was to develop in Britain.

The Scottish pattern of education for the ministry is for candidates to be trained in the universities. In Edinburgh, James Blackie (who had organized the first SPA Easter conferences) was appointed lecturer and, soon afterwards, Professor of Christian Ethics and Practical Theology. He was joined by Alastair V. Campbell, an Edinburgh graduate who had recently completed a Doctorate in Pastoral Counselling in San Francisco. He began to introduce pastoral counselling as part of undergraduate courses. In 1970–1 the three full-time chaplaincies in Edinburgh hospitals became vacant and in (what was then) a unique arrangement involving the Church of Scotland, the Lothian Health Board and the university the three new chaplains were also given honorary university appointments with responsibilities for developing supervised hospital placements as part of the courses being taught by Alastair Campbell.

The Churches

Within the Churches themselves, professionalism in pastoral care began to be taken more seriously. One arena where this had to be so was in hospital chaplaincy. Previously this area of work had been viewed (at least by some) as a dumping ground for old men and misfits who could no longer function in a parish. But in a National Health Service that was increasingly secular, professional and technological, this pattern of chaplaincy was no longer viable. The Church of England Hospital Chaplaincies Council, first under Norman Autton and then under Eric Reid, began to take training more seriously. They instituted a number of in-service courses and vacation courses for theological students. Many chaplains ministering in situations of acute human need found themselves doing so on the boundaries of their personal and professional skills. They began to seek out further training sometimes within the growing body of secular agencies offering training in psychotherapy. Several of these chaplains, as well as establishing well-respected departments within their own hospitals, also made significant contributions to the growing British literature on pastoral care and counselling. Derek Blows, one-time Chaplain at Warlingham Park Hospital in Surrey, edited the SPCK's New Library of Pastoral Care. Among the chaplains who contributed to that series were Ian Ainsworth-Smith of St George's Hospital (1982), Peter Speck of the Royal Free (1982 and 1988) and John Foskett of the Maudesley Hospital (1984 and 1988).

This period also witnessed within some Anglican dioceses the appointment of Advisors in Pastoral Care and Counselling. These men (and later women too) became important resources for training in counselling in their own areas. They usually functioned on an ecumenical basis and increasingly they fostered the skills of lay people as much as those of the clergy. This development, as we shall see, has had important consequences for the development of pastoral counselling in Britain.

The coming of the counsellors

So far I have drawn attention to some of the influences that have shaped new approaches to pastoral care in Britain. Few of the developments described began with the intention of training pastoral counsellors. Most saw what they were doing as an enhancement of the pastoral skills of those already involved in, or about to enter, ministry. I must now examine the contribution of some organizations that were established with the definite aim of offering counselling services and/or training in counselling.

The **Clinical Theology Association,** founded by Dr Frank Lake in 1962, was one of the first to be established. While Superintendent of the Christian Medical College at Vellore in South India, Lake became interested in dynamic psychiatry. He returned to England to undertake a Diploma in Psychological Medicine at Leeds where he came under the influence of Harry Guntrip. At the request of some of the English Bishops, Lake began to offer courses on pastoral care and counselling; these courses consisted of a three-hour seminar every three weeks for two years.

Initially, the stated aims were 'The furtherance of training within the C of E and other member churches of the WCC in pastoral care in general, and especially of those whose concern is with persons suffering from spiritual and emotional distress, from psychoneurotic and psychotic illness and from personality disorders and the like and the provision of the facilities for such care and counselling'. These were ambitious aims and Clinical Theology was not without its critics. Hugh Melinsky wrote:

> Its very title was disliked by some theologians as presuming to offer *the only* system of pastoral care, whereas both its theology and its psychology were drawn from selected portions of these very large fields. For theological guidance, Dr Lake looks principally to Job, St John's Gospel, St Paul's Epistle to the Romans, St John of the Cross, Kierkegaard, Simone Weil and Martin Buber. His psychological mentors are Freud and the neo-Freudians, Klein, Fairbairn, Sullivan and Guntrip. Since there are great divergences amongst theologians and psychiatrists in their own fields, it is hardly to be expected that any one mortal could lead

these two contentious disciplines to a happy marriage. The period
of courtship looks like being a long one.

(Melinsky 1970: 119)

Twenty-five years on, few would wish to argue that the marriage
has actually taken place, though the two disciplines are certainly
still living together. Lake was a charismatic character and a genius
with a great facility for words: his magnum opus, *Clinical Theology*
(1966) ran to nearly 1200 pages. This book sets out his analysis of
the depressive, hysteric and schizoid personality traits, locating the
formation of each in the earliest experiences of life, sometimes in
the process of being born itself. His later work was even more
controversial with its emphasis upon the 'Maternal-Foetal Distress
Syndrome' (1981). His belief was that much psychic trauma found
its origin in events in the life of the mother which had a significant
effect on the foetus during the first three months of pregnancy.

Since 1959 many thousands of clergy and lay people have participated in and benefited from Clinical Theology seminars. For some
clergy they remedied deficiencies in past theological training. It
provided them with a vocabulary and a conceptual framework for
understanding both their pastoral relationships and themselves.
Sometimes the seminars provided a safe haven for unburdening a
pastoral load that had become almost too heavy to carry alone. And
even if they were not prepared to accept all the connections Lake
made between psychology and theology, it was at least an introduction to the possibility of making such links. The programme demonstrated how academic theology could become alive. For many lay
people, particularly those working in the caring professions, Clinical
Theology helped them understand their work in a Christian perspective. One by-product was that the pastoral task was affirmed
as belonging to the whole Church, not just to those who were
ordained to the ministry of word and sacrament.

Among the other organizations that set out to promote counselling in the pastoral/spiritual context, none has achieved more than
the **Westminster Pastoral Foundation**. In 1965, Bill Kyle, a Methodist minister, proposed the setting-up in London of 'a church-
cum-centre in which the whole ministry of the church would be
concerned with pastoral counselling. This would include both "normal counselling" and more long-term care than is possible in the
local circuit church' (Black 1991: 6). Earlier, in 1960, Kyle had
founded the Highgate Counselling Centre in North London based
on a local church. One result of that experience was to heighten

awareness of the potential of lay people, particularly women, for pastoral work. Kyle's 1965 proposal was much more ambitious, anticipating the need for a centre of national excellence. It found embodiment in a suite of rooms in Central Hall, Westminster, close to the Abbey and the Houses of Parliament. Before beginning in earnest Kyle went to study in the United States, first at the Academy of Religion and Psychiatry in New York, and then at Andover Newton Theological School in Boston. Since 1969 WPF has grown to the extent that in 1990, for example, the typical counselling load was 650 interviews per week. It has also developed a highly sophisticated training programme with its own standards of certification. A national network of about fifty affiliated and associated pastoral counselling centres has come into being, each one either having met, or working towards, standards of accreditation set by WPF. In later chapters I will explore issues in the development of WPF that have wider implications for the understanding of pastoral counselling itself, in particular its growing struggle to come to an agreed position about the nature of the 'pastoral' dimension of its work. Meanwhile, we should note that while WPF was certainly the largest organization in the field, it was not the only one.

In 1971, the **Dympna Centre** was founded in London by Father Louis Marteau, a Roman Catholic priest. It had three declared aims. First, it set out to provide counselling for those whose emotional and personal problems arose within the context of their religious faith. As such, it saw itself as having a distinctive role, providing pastoral support for priests and members of religious orders. Second, it sought to provide an advisory and consultative service for those in pastoral work who needed expertise in the field of mental health. Finally, it sought to provide advanced training in counselling for those with a basic training or experience in human relationships.

While the Dympna Centre was a Catholic foundation, its influence was ecumenical. In a *Contact* article, Irene Bloomfield (1991: 17–23) describes how those early participants in the Centre were themselves subsequently instrumental in setting up counselling centres within different religious traditions. Bloomfield herself and Rabbi Danny Smith were co-founders of the Jewish Raphael Centre. Harry Dean became Director of Salvation Army Counselling Services; within the Catholic tradition the Jesuit Jim Christie established the Garnethill Centre in Glasgow. Micael O'Regan, a Dominican, became Director of Eckhart House in Dublin. It is important to emphasize the ecumenical nature of the pastoral counselling movement. Bloomfield quotes one Catholic participant as saying:

I learned experimentally that the religious divide was not so much between different traditions and denominations but rather between different sensibilities, which crossed the traditions and denominations. I frequently felt more at home with a Rabbi than a Christian.

(Bloomfield 1991: 20)

When pastoral counsellors disagreed, it was more likely to be about schools of psychotherapy than religion! This undoubtedly had positive aspects both in furthering understanding at the denominational level and in terms of the personal freedom and new horizons for individuals. It can be argued, however, that in the excitement of the psychotherapeutic journey the religious issues have simply been glossed over and have to be confronted at another point – as I shall do in Chapter Four.

THE PRESSURES FOR A NATIONAL PASTORAL ORGANIZATION

This brief history shows how within a short space of time there developed a number of organizations concerned directly or indirectly with the advancement of counselling broadly within the Judaeo-Christian tradition. Almost inevitably voices were raised urging the setting-up of a central body, which at least would serve as a focus of communication between these diverse enterprises. Perhaps eventually it would begin to set agreed standards of professional practice. It is possible to identify a number of reasons that led to this pressure for a national body:

1 It was not only in the pastoral field that counselling was gaining increased prominence. A number of voluntary organizations were already established offering counselling in specific 'problem' areas (for example the Marriage Guidance Council, as it was then called, and Cruse which offered support to the bereaved). Increasingly, both full-time and part-time courses were being offered by educational institutions, particularly the Polytechnics. In 1971 the Standing Conference for the Advancement of Counselling was formed to bring together the various statutary and voluntary organizations. If the various pastoral counselling agencies were to be represented on this body (which was the forerunner of the British Association for Counselling) it was obviously important that they should co-ordinate their endeavours.

2 Increasingly those being trained by the pastoral counselling centres were lay people, particularly women. In a sense the clergy
did not need accreditation because ordination gave them licence
to practise whatever new skills they were acquiring. But lay people
who had undergone training enjoyed no such benefit. They needed
some external (preferably national) certification, especially if they
wished to offer their services for a fee. Only a national body could
provide this. Indeed, following the Foster Report on Scientology
in 1971 it was widely expected that no one would be permitted
to offer counselling or psychotherapeutic services who was not
accredited by a responsible body.

3 Finally there was the transatlantic experience: the American Association of Pastoral Counselors appeared to offer benefits to its
members.

At the time when pressures were building up for a national pastoral organization, one voice was raised in protest. Robert Lambourne
was one of the founders of the Birmingham University Diploma in
Pastoral Studies. A medical doctor, he tried to integrate his Christian belief with his daily work. He resigned from General Practice
in order to undertake a BD degree by thesis. His thesis was followed
by further study which led to a Diploma in Psychological Medicine.
It is in the context of Lambourne's medical background (and that
of his colleague Michael Wilson) that we must understand the Birmingham protest against what they saw as the growing medical
captivity of pastoral counselling. A visit to the United States was
followed by a paper (1970) in which Lambourne both deplored 'the
total lack of theological thrust in the so-called dialogue with psychoanalysis' (1970: 132). He noted that 'the unparalleled American
sophistication in the training of hospital chaplains has been so
entangled in counselling that it has rarely if ever said anything
prophetic about the medical structures within which it counselled'
(1970: 134). Lambourne, therefore, was not enthusiastic about the
pressure to set up a national pastoral organization in Britain. He
expressed his arguments in a paper in *Contact* (1971: 25); this sums
up his position:

My thesis, however, is that the pastoral counselling called for
in this country during the next twenty years cannot be built
around a practice and a conceptual framework derived from
professional problem-solving and prevention of breakdown. That
practice and conceptual framework is based upon the clinical,
medical and psychoanalytic models of the USA of twenty years
ago, and it has proved inadequate. To copy it, even with many

modificatons would be a disaster, because not only is it not what is wanted but also because it will be an obstacle to what is wanted. An accredited hierarchical pastoral movement will be professional, problem solving or problem preventing, standardised and defined. What is required is pastoral care which is lay, corporate, adventurous, variegated and diffuse.

This article drew a response from Howard Clinebell (1971: 26–9). While agreeing with much of what Lambourne had written, particularly with regard to the last sentence in the above quotation, Clinebell felt that a false dichotomy had been drawn between lay and professional pastoral care. His response may have been the result of seeing the British debate through American eyes. In the USA, ordination is a prerequisite for accreditation as a pastoral counsellor and so 'lay' pastoral care cannot be 'professional'. In Britain pastoral counsellors can be both lay and professional.

In the event, the Association for Pastoral Care and Counselling came into being, later becoming a Division of the British Association of Counselling, though it can be argued that Lambourne's critique did have an influence upon the issues that became important in APCC. In recent years APCC has participated in a developing international and European movement and, as we shall see, issues that were important to APCC were fed into that movement (Lyall 1993).

This historical survey has fallen mainly within one particular theological tradition, namely that of liberal Protestantism. Yet a consideration of counselling in the context of contemporary spirituality must also take into account other significant developments. The conservative-evangelical strand within Christianity has given birth to a somewhat different approach to counselling. This approach is much more avowedly Christian in its orientation and makes a more explicit use of Biblical language and ideas in the counselling process. In the next chapter I shall compare the distinctive insights of the 'Christian' counsellors and the 'pastoral' counsellors.

There are two further ways in which our concern must be enlarged. While a brief reference has been made to counselling in the Jewish tradition, we must also recognize the pluralism of religious belief in modern society and that other religions outwith the Judaeo-Christian tradition have their own distinctive understandings of what it means to care for a fellow human being. We must also take account of another aspect of the current situation. It is a paradox of our time that in the midst of a society which is supposed to be increasingly secular and materialistic, there has been a revival of interest in what is broadly called 'spirituality'. Sometimes this interest finds a traditional expression within the historic religious communities. At other times, apparently divorced from any community of faith, the search for an authentic spirituality takes a more individualistic form, a search for personal fulfilment. All these phenomena constitute the pastoral/religious/spiritual context in which counselling takes place, and will be discussed in the next chapter.

· TWO ·

Counselling in the pastoral and spiritual context

It is a common misconception in the use of the word 'spiritual' that it is of relevance only within the life of the Church. That the search for an authentic spirituality is – or ought to be – a concern of the Church is not to be doubted. However, in order to understand the complexity of counselling in a spiritual or pastoral context, we need to broaden our horizons to encompass a view that includes counselling not only within the Church but within other religious traditions, as well as in the context of a more general spiritual quest on the part of humankind. Even within the pastoral context of the Church itself, there is the question of the distinction, which must be examined, between counselling from a general religious perspective and a more specifically Christian approach to counselling.

The chief characteristic of pastoral counselling in the context of this book is its close relationship to a number of different kinds of care and support systems within the Church. At the simplest level (and not necessarily the least effective) there is the befriending and mutual sharing of concerns which simply happens within many, if not most, congregations. Then there is the routine pastoral care exercised by ministers and priests as they go about their official tasks of baptizing, marrying and burying, of visiting the housebound and the elderly, of leading worship and preaching, of conducting meetings and involving themselves in their communities. As I described in the last chapter, theological education is now designed to enable clergy to carry out these tasks with a degree of psychological knowledge and insight. Increasingly, lay people are setting out to acquire the listening skills to enable them to share more effectively in this ministry of pastoral care. At a deeper level still there is the pastoral counselling which is the main focus of this study and it will be necessary to explore the relationship between pastoral counselling and pastoral care. Finally, we should note that a distinction is sometimes made between pastoral counselling and psychotherapy and to this issue I shall also return.

Pastoral counselling and pastoral care

Historically, counselling within the Church has normally been an expression of its ministry of pastoral care. The emergence of a separate breed of specially trained pastoral counsellors is a comparatively recent phenomenon.

An attempt has been made elsewhere (Foskett and Lyall 1988: 108–12) to explore the differences and the relationship between these two ministries. Generally speaking, in pastoral care it is the pastor who makes the first approach, responding to perceived human need as part of an on-going ministry, while in counselling it is the parishioner or client who takes the initiative. Again, pastoral counselling is nearly always more structured as regards both place and time compared, with pastoral care. This means that pastoral counselling is characterized by the negotiation of an explicit contract, while in pastoral care any contract, if it exists at all, will be of a more implicit nature. Further, psychodynamic issues are handled somewhat differently. In a pastoral care relationship, the pastor hesitates before addressing the matter of resistance, while the more explicit contracts of pastoral counselling permit this to happen. Again, while someone trained in pastoral care must be aware of the fact that transference and countertransference may affect the pastoral relationship, the pastoral counsellor should be much more skilled in dealing with these phenomena. It is comparatively easy to discuss this distinction in a theoretical way – much easier than to keep them separate in practice. What begins as pastoral care may soon develop into a counselling relationship ('Could we meet to talk about this at greater length?'). Then the pastor needs to be aware of the changed dynamics of the relationship. There is some debate about whether a minister can be a counsellor to a member of his or her congregation; I shall return to this issue in the next chapter.

In comparing pastoral care and pastoral counselling, it should not be thought that pastoral care is in any sense inferior or less important. Pastoral care has its own integrity. John Patton, one of America's leading authorities on pastoral counselling, has recently written *Pastoral Care in Context: An Introduction to Pastoral Care* (1993: 4) in which he affirms the primacy of pastoral care as a ministry of the Church. In this book he moves beyond 'classical' and 'clinical pastoral'

paradigms to what he describes as the 'communal contextual', emphasizing the caring community and the various contexts for care,
rather than focusing upon pastoral care as the work of the ordained
ministry. The emphasis in the classical model was upon the *message* of
pastoral care, namely the love of God, and the focus of the clinical
pastoral model upon the *personhood* of those involved in giving and
receiving the message of care. The communal contextual model
does not negate these emphases but preserves the best features of
both in an approach which is less critically individualistic than previous models. Indeed, it could be argued that one of the distinctive
strengths of pastoral counselling is that it takes place within the
wider context of pastoral care with the potential support of a caring
community. A good example of this is to be found in the Bereavement Care teams set up in some congregations. Few people depart
this life without a funeral service conducted by a minister or priest.
This can form a considerable proportion of the work of ministers
especially in the Church of Scotland and Church of England where
people, even those with no involvement in the Church, look to
their parish church at such a time. Most ministers would like to
provide more support and follow-up than other duties allow. Yet it
could be argued that the sensitive management of grief is one the
Church's main contributions to community mental health. Increasingly, groups of lay people, appropriately chosen, trained and supported, provide support for the bereaved either concurrently with
the pastoral care provided by the minister or in the following months.

Pastoral counselling and psychotherapy

In the counselling/therapy world as a whole there is confusion
about the similarities and differences between counselling and psychotherapy. In his book *Pastoral Psychotherapy* Carroll Wise blurs any
difference between these two activities:

> The work of the pastor has usually been called pastoral
> counseling . . . However in this book we shall discard the use of
> this term. Both in a broad and a more narrow sense, the pastor
> does a form of psychotherapy.
>
> (Wise 1980: 2)

Normally, however, some clear distinctions are drawn between
counselling and therapy both in terms of the nature of the problems
encountered in the client and the skills required of the counsellor
or therapist. Psychotherapy is likely to be deemed appropriate for

the client whose problems are more deep-rooted, verging on the pathological and leading to an inability to function normally. Psychotherapists require a correspondingly greater level of skill and training, enabling them to work with clients at a deeper level over a longer period of time, with the ability to deal with unconscious material. This therapeutic approach may include the integration of symbols from within the unconscious and may make a considerable difference when working in a religious context, where symbols are about, but are not always understood by clients as pointing to their inner world as much as to a spiritual realm.

The physical context

The issue of context is further complicated when we consider the various settings in which pastoral counselling takes place. Traditionally the locus of most pastoral counselling has been the local parish or congregation. Post-funeral visits may develop into a deeper kind of grief counselling; a member of the congregation abandoned by a spouse may seek help to come to terms with that loss; visits to the terminally ill may lead to deeper explorations of the meaning of life. People will tell their minister about being made redundant, or coping with an alcoholic spouse or rebellious teenagers. Whether or not they come asking for counselling, the minister must have counselling skills in order to respond effectively.

However, there are other settings beyond the parish in which pastoral counselling takes place. We have already noted that the Westminster Pastoral Foundation has a network of some fifty affiliated or associated centres spread around Britain. (Affiliated centres have already met standards laid down by WPF, associated centres are committed to moving towards these standards.) These centres offer both training and counselling. The trainees are predominantly lay and mostly women. Clients are either self-referred or may be referred by others, such as ministers or doctors, either because the relevant skills are not available locally or because there are clear advantages for the client in being given help within the relative anonymity of the counselling centre. Although many of these trainees have a Christian faith and view counselling as a specific form of Christian service, it cannot be assumed that this is always the case. My impression is that many trainees are quite agnostic in their religious views but enrol in courses because the training is good, particularly when accredited by an organization such as WPF. However, it is also possible, as I indicate later, that some people become involved in this kind of counselling as way of finding satisfaction in the perennial human quest for meaning and purpose, especially when that quest has not been satisfied through more orthodox religious channels.

In recent years there has been an expansion of the role of ministry in non-parochial settings. Industry, higher education, prisons and hospitals have all seen the appointment of chaplains, of different religious traditions (and not just Christian), both full-time or part-time. Each of these secular arenas has required its own style of chaplaincy that can respond to a distinctive agenda and ethos. What all these ministries have in common is the need for chaplains to be pastorally available. This can lead to counselling relationships of some depth. When I was a full-time hospital chaplain, much of my ministry was one of pastoral care, visiting patients on the wards, recognizing when to stop by a bedside and knowing when to move on, asking how people were, listening for the hidden anxieties behind the cheerful answer, 'I'm fine'. In fifteen years of this work I never ceased to be surprised at the depth of some of these brief pastoral encounters. The very vulnerability of some of the patients seemed to provoke a desire to explore matters of great importance. How can a good God allow so much suffering? What if all these tests show up something nasty? What will life be like after I lose my leg? How will my family cope without me? The pastoral task was to enable the patient to explore these issues to the extent that they seemed willing to do so within the limits of their physical weakness and emotional vulnerability.

Other counselling situations frequently presented themselves. One involved relatives agonizing over a decision to allow the kidneys of a brain-damaged son, daughter or parent to be used for transplantation. On other occasions, the Department of Psychiatry referred patients where their own involvement with them had revealed a religious dimension to the problem. Was one patient's conviction that God was speaking to him within the range of normal religious behaviour or an indication of psychotic illness? Was a Baptist girl of twenty who did not sleep with her fiancé suffering from arrested sexual development or was she simply observing the norms of her own religious group? There were never easy answers, but sometimes it fell to the chaplain to affirm the normality of religious experience in a setting where many professionals did not regard it as other than pathological. Sometimes staff themselves wanted to talk with the chaplain, either because they had no minister of their own, or because they preferred the relative anonymity of the work environment compared with the local parish, or because they wanted to talk about a work-related problem. The ethical issues generated by new medical technologies gave rise to many problems which straddled the boundary between the professional and the personal. Could a nurse opposed in principle to abortion still be involved in the aftercare of the patient? To what extent was it right to use new technology to keep patients alive when the quality of life was awful and the prospects for recovery nil? Sometimes these conversations took place in the duty-room, sometimes in the dining-room and sometimes in the chaplain's office. All these examples of my own reflect the opportunity for counselling in specialized pastoral settings.

But the point I wish to emphasize is that frequently in the pastoral context, counselling does not fit easily into structures which are regarded as normal in other contexts. Clinebell writes:

> The 'structure' of formal counseling – appointments, definite time limits, a private meeting place – are often missing. It is important for a pastor to discover that these features of the 'fifty-minute hour' are not essential to helping people with their inner problems in significant ways. The minister who makes the structured interview his primary operational model will miss many of his finest counseling opportunities.
>
> (Clinebell 1966: 29)

Of course there are other settings in which counselling or psychotherapy does conform more closely in its practice to the working norms of the discipline. Of particular interest is the work of Heronbrook House at Knowle, near Birmingham. Heronbrook House is a Roman Catholic foundation established in 1978 by the Sisters of Charity of St Paul. Its declared aim is 'to help priests and religious to become fully integrated persons in the context of their unique calling and commitment to Christ. To this end those experiencing difficulties have an opportunity at Heronbrook House to live in a therapeutic community.' Under the directorship of Dr Breda O'Sullivan, it offers a residential programme of group and individual psychotherapy as well as ancillary therapies of a creative and expressive nature such as art, ceramics, yoga, psychodrama and movement therapy. There is also a lecture programme in psychology, spirituality and psychotheology. What is particularly impressive about Heronbrook House is that as well as working with the highest psychotherapeutic standards, the life of the community centres around the Eucharist celebrated daily in the superb modern chapel. The Eucharist is the setting in which new guests are welcomed into the community and from which they take their leave.

This is certainly a definite expression of counselling in the pastoral/ spiritual context; later I shall consider the wider implications of this work.

What makes counselling 'pastoral'?

A further complexity in relation to counselling in a pastoral setting relates to the various connotations of the word 'pastoral'. Sometimes it is used in primarily secular contexts, for example in the relation to the work of Guidance teachers in schools or of Directors of Studies in universities. In such contexts the word refers to the personal dimensions of their work against the purely academic.

Even in overtly religious contexts, at least four different understandings of the significance of the pastoral dimension can be identified.

1 Pastoral counselling is counselling offered by an ordained minister. Here the emphasis is on the ecclesiastical status of the counsellor. The counselling is pastoral because the pastor has been designated as such by some religious body. It is interesting to note that while ordination is not a sufficient condition for membership of the American Association of Pastoral Counselors, it is certainly a necessary condition. This is in sharp contrast to the British scene where the majority of people who train as counsellors in such organizations as the Westminster Pastoral Foundation or Clinical Theology or the St John's College, Nottingham, Diploma in Pastoral Counselling are not ordained but lay.

2 Pastoral counselling is counselling offered within a community of faith. This was the view of Robert Lambourne who, as I showed in the last chapter, was suspicious of the individualistic and psychoanalytic models which he saw as a threat to the development of pastoral counselling in Britain. Lambourne was not opposed to high professional standards for counsellors – he himself was a highly competent psychotherapist. But for him pastoral counselling belonged within the Church, and indeed was of the essence of the communal life of the Church:

> To state the argument very strongly, pastoral care, of which pastoral counselling is a part, is separated from its very life unless it is substantially concerned with the holiness-in-service of the church, as koinonia [community/fellowship] rather than being preoccupied with the ego-formation, identity righteousness, or salvation of its individual members.
>
> (Lambourne 1974: 31)

3 What makes counselling pastoral is the frame of reference of the
   pastor. This view is expressed by Wayne Oates, a leading American writer:

> On another occasion, a psychiatric resident asked me in a
> case conference, 'What is it that you do as a minister in
> relation to a patient that I as a psychiatrist do not do?' I
> replied: 'You have a choice as to whether or not you bring
> God into the focus of the patient's attention. I am different in
> that if I am introduced as a minister, I have no choice but that
> God tacitly or overtly becomes the focus of the relationship.'
>
> (Oates 1974: 12)

Since in this case God is on the agenda of the counsellor who
assumes that it is also on the client's, this will undoubtedly have
an effect on the course of the pastoral conversation.

Whether or not we can go along with Oates at this point, it
must be acknowledged that he does point to an important truth
which is related to the client's internal frame of reference. If the
counsellor is introduced as a minister or pastor, or if the counselling takes place in a setting which has an overt church connection or which describes itself as 'pastoral', this will have
consequences for the counselling process. For the client will bring
to the counselling relationship all his or her past experiences,
good and bad, of God, Church and ministers and priests. These
transference phenomena may need to be brought into the open
at an early stage.

4 What makes a conversation pastoral is its content. We find this
   view explicitly stated by the Swiss Reformed pastoral theologian,
   Eduard Thurneysen:

> pastoral conversation has as its only content the communica-
> tion of the forgiveness of sins in Jesus Christ.
>
> (Thurneysen 1962: 147)

It is perhaps unfair to use this quotation out of context because
elsewhere Thurneysen certainly points to the need for pastoral
care to be grounded in the ability to *listen*. He also affirms the
contributions of psychology and psychotherapy as 'auxiliary sciences' in the healing of persons. But he is a good example of
those who would define pastoral counselling in terms of its explicitly Christian themes and language.

In discussing the meaning of the word 'pastoral', I have demonstrated the wide variety of understandings of the word which exist

in practice. However, within the context of the Christian Church in particular, there is one further distinction which must be considered in some detail.

PASTORAL COUNSELLING AND CHRISTIAN COUNSELLING

I have outlined above some explicitly Christian understandings of the word 'pastoral'. In view of this, it might be thought that I am being somewhat pedantic, or even perverse, in introducing the distinction encapsulated in the title of this section. However, I hope to show that within the Church there is another approach to counselling which is different in its ethos and nuances from any of the definitions of the pastoral counselling I have just described.

A feature of the life of the Church in the twentieth century has been the tension between liberals and conservatives. This has manifested itself in various ways. Most fundamentally, with regard to the interpretation of the Bible, the more conservative groups have resisted the insights of modern scholarship, believing that to cast doubt on the literal truth of Scripture is to threaten the very foundations of faith itself. Nor did Freud's views on the origins of religious belief endear him to conservative Christians who could only respond negatively to his view of religion as an illusion with no future. Finally, Freudian psychology appeared to lead to a relativizing of ethical values, particularly in the sexual realm. This was obviously unacceptable to the upholders of what were regarded as traditional Christian values.

The approaches to pastoral counselling so far described have largely been developed within the framework of the liberal Protestantism of the early twentieth century. Even Thurneysen, though he sounds rather conservative and directive in his approach to people, comes from a Reformed tradition which has embraced the results of modern biblical scholarship. Pastors in the more liberal churches have felt able to engage in dialogue with the new secular therapies even though the outcome at first sight sometimes appears to be inconsistent with traditional Christian understandings of the nature of humankind. For this reason the initial response of evangelicals was to distance themselves from the pastoral counselling movement. Recent years, however, have seen the rapid growth of alternative approaches to counselling which are more explicitly biblical in their orientation and methods. It is interesting to speculate about the reasons for this development. Perhaps it was simply that with the emergence of a more psychologically sophisticated society and of the acceptance of counselling within the Church, the evangelicals had to provide their own alternative.

Narramore (1990: 151) distinguishes three uses of the term 'Christian psychotherapist':

1 *Any therapist who is a Christian.* In this case, there is no explicit use of Christian resources in the process of counselling. The faith of the counsellor is reflected in care for and sensitivity to all the client's needs and concerns, including the spiritual. This understanding of what it means to be a Christian psychotherapist does not differ significantly from that of the pastoral counselling already described.

2 *A therapist who conceptualizes the counselling process in terms of Christian concepts and values.* Here, while there may be no explicit use of biblical material in the counselling itself, the counsellor may consider the relationship between (for example) psychopathology and scriptural teaching about sin, or about the nature of personal responsibility, and this may in turn influence how the counsellor handles emotions like guilt and anger.

3 *A therapist who actively incorporates biblical principles and concepts within the therapeutic process.* Narramore (1990: 152) summarizes the character of this group very well:

> The third group of therapists goes beyond conceptualising the therapeutic process in Christian terms to actively verbalising the patients' struggles in Christian (or biblical) terms. These therapists may draw on specific biblical passages and principles in helping patients come to grips with the origin, nature and resolution of their adjustment problems. They may bring relevant scriptures to bear on problems such as guilt and forgiveness, marriage and divorce, self-esteem and interpersonal conflicts. This group of therapists includes a diverse collection of individuals ranging from very directive and didactic therapists to those who utilise an insight-oriented depth therapy. Their commonality is found not in their therapeutic orientation or style but in their incorporation of biblical principles in their therapeutic endeavours.

As Narramore has indicated, there are wide differences even within this third category. Lawrence Crabb (1975, 1977) in the United States and Selwyn Hughes (1981) in Britain are prepared to draw on the insights of secular psychology where these do not contradict what they believe to be scriptural truth. A different approach is to be found in the 'nouthetic counselling' of the American Jay Adams. The Greek verb *noutheteo* means 'to admonish' and the basic technique of this approach is the use of scripture to change behaviour. A key biblical text is II Timothy 3: 16 'All scripture is inspired by God and profitable for teaching, for reproof, for correction, and for training in righteousness' (RSV). Behaviour has primacy over feeling. Indeed, since the existence of personal emotional problems is discounted, there is no place for an approach to psychotherapy which is directed towards the relief of such problems.

> Biblically, there is no warrant for acknowledging the existence of a separate and distinct discipline called psychiatry. There are in the Scriptures only three specified sources of personal problems in living: demonic activity (principally possession), personal sin and organic illness. These three are interrelated. All options are covered by these three heads, leaving no room for a third: non-organic mental illness.
>
> (Adams 1973: 9)

This is an extreme position which has been subject to searching critique even by counsellors of an evangelical persuasion. Roger Hurding, one of the most respected exponents of Christian counselling in Britain, writes:

> In choosing the 'nouthetic' words (*noutheteo* occurring eight times, *nouthesia* three times in the New Testament, and neglecting a range of alternatives, including *parakaleo* (109 occurrences) and *paraklesis* (twenty-nine times)), Adams seems to favour the more directive and admonishing stance of the former to the more encouraging and consoling style of the latter.
>
> (Hurding 1985: 288)

Hurding later points out (1985: 392) that the sense of the Greek noun *paraklesis* is much more of a God who comes alongside us in a time of need with very different implications for a biblical understanding of counselling. In a later book, Hurding, himself a medical practitioner, affirms the importance of an understanding of psychological understanding:

> With respect to psychological mechanisms, would-be counsellors need at least a measure of understanding of the inner conflicts, mixed motives, insecurities and resistances to change that govern the lives of many of those they will counsel, as well as their own. In fact these two perspectives are inseparable: true self-understanding is impossible without genuine relating

to others, and a valid appreciation of other people is hamstrung where there is little or no self-awareness.

(Hurding 1992: 66)

Hurding has been one of those engaged in the setting-up of the Association of Christian Counsellors, an organization established to ensure that Christian counsellors work to professional standards recognized by secular counselling organizations. In two articles in the journal *The Christian Counsellor* (I: 4, Autumn 1991 and II: 2, Spring 1992) details are given of this evolving organization, with an emphasis on the need to accredit training programmes, counsellors and supervisors. While acknowledging the role of the British Association of Counselling in the accreditation of counsellors, it is rather curious that in seeing the need for a Christian accrediting body, no mention is made of the work of the Association for Pastoral Care and Counselling which is part of BAC.

The above journal, renamed *Care and Counsel* in 1993, is well produced. Its Executive Editor is Selwyn Hughes. While addressing human problems within a biblical perspective, the problems themselves are usually accurately analysed in psychological terms and demonstrate an awareness of the danger of solutions which are too directive or which arise out of the inner needs of the counsellor.

The Christian counselling movement raises issues which are important for all who counsel in the context of religious and spiritual values and beliefs. These issues concern the extent to which these values and beliefs should be excluded from the counselling process, and indeed whether they can be. I shall return to this matter in Chapter Four where I attempt to address issues specific to counselling in the pastoral and spiritual context. Meanwhile we must recognize that this context stretches far beyond Christianity and explore the forms of mutual help and support that exist within other religious traditions.

CARE AND COUNSELLING IN OTHER RELIGIOUS TRADITIONS

I have in my possession a list of over sixty London-based counselling organizations which offer their services in the context of the diverse ethnic, cultural and religious groups within the city. While it would be fascinating to explore the philosophy and methods of each of these organizations, and the extent to which these are a reflection of their different religious backgrounds, that exercise lies beyond the scope of this volume. There is, however, a related enterprise which may be of some value: to investigate whether there is something corresponding to the Christian pastoral tradition in the other great world religions that lie behind many of these counselling organizations. I propose to examine briefly four such religions: Judaism, Islam, Hinduism and Buddhism. We shall be concerned not only with the ways in which personal support has traditionally been manifest within these communities of faith but also with the extent to which the practice of counselling finds a contemporary expression.

Judaism

In his *Pastoral Care and the Jewish Tradition*, Rabbi Robert Katz points out that counselling has not, until comparatively recently, been a feature of the rabbinic ministry:

> Unlike Christian pastors, we have not had the model of Jesus the Good Shepherd, the Pastor. It is not in the nature of Judaism to enshrine a single person as the focus of theology. Among Jews it is the Torah, containing the essence of our faith, that is central, energizing, and formative. In place of a charismatic person to emulate, Jews follow the principle of *imitatio Dei*; to emulate God is incumbent upon all Jews, lay or rabbinic.
>
> (Katz 1985: 18)

For Grollman (1990), it is the family that provides stability for the Jew, the home being the centre of ritual, and the parents, by their example, being the primary teachers of the faith. Grollman identifies several features of Judaism which, he believes, have helped the Jewish family withstand many of the disruptive influences of modern life. These are a healthy attitude towards sex, a faith that can rejoice in the good things of this world, well-defined rituals for meeting death, a healthy respect for education, a high concept of social justice and a positive approach to medicine.

While rabbis have traditionally been teachers of the Torah, there has also always been, within their interpretation of the law, much psychological wisdom. This has been particularly true of two movements within Judaism. The *musar* movement founded by Rabbi Israel Salanter in the nineteenth century used certain psychological techniques, usually in a group setting, to bring about moral improvement in individuals. Katz (1985: 71) identifies Salanter as having an intuitive appreciation of factors which today we would call psychodynamic. For Salanter, the emotions, the 'dim area', were more compelling than reason, the 'bright area', but the emotions had to be mastered so that individuals were set free to engage in acts of practical morality.

In a second movement within Judaism, Katz finds parallels with the modern person-centred approach to counselling (1985: 75). The Hasidic movement grew out of the persecution and ostracism of the Jews in eighteenth-century Eastern Europe. It was an attempt to respond to the needs of ordinary Jews with a religion that helped them make sense of their intolerable position. Baal Shem Tov, brought up in the Jewish mystical tradition, taught that in the midst of despair there were more immediate ways to God than through great learning and long prayers. Mills captures the essence of the Hasidic movement thus:

> What the Baal Shem Tov brought to a dispirited people was a hope of a life unified in all its parts, personal, interpersonal and metaphysical . . . By utilizing classical mystical concepts, he insisted that the separations they experienced between good and evil, rich and poor, male and female, mercy and judgement, all their inner and outer contradictions contained holy sparks separated from their true source in God . . . The task of the Hasidic master or *rebbe* was to gather up these fallen sparks everywhere.
>
> (Mills 1990: 495)

At the heart of this movement was a meeting or *yehidut* between *rebbe* and disciple which was remarkably similar to a modern counselling relationship. These meetings took place regularly and at times of crisis:

> We can find many features akin to psychotherapy in the personal encounter between the master and the Hasid. Unlike the sages of the Talmud the rebbe was not concerned with the encounters as vehicles for teaching. He was involved in a therapeutic system. The advice he gave was often grounded in biblical and rabbinic wisdom, but the goal was salvific. Cure came about through face-to-face contact between a charismatic personality and an individual Jew who felt free to come for personal help with any problem of living.
>
> (Katz 1985: 73)

Grollman (1990: 496) notes Martin Buber's acknowledgement of the influence of the *yehidut*, the sacred encounter between *rebbe* and Hasid, in his formulation of the 'I–Thou' relationship over against what he called the 'I–It' relationship. This has been important in conceptualizing the process of psychotherapy because the I–Thou relationship is essentially one of openness and mutuality whereas the I–It relationship is manipulative and self-satisfying.

Elsewhere (1987: 196) Katz has drawn attention to the fact that nearly all Jewish seminaries now offer courses in counselling. He believes that the model of the Christian pastor has had its effect on the Jewish clergy. What is certain is that from Freud onwards, Jews have been prominent in the development of psychoanalysis. In a recent collection of essays exploring the relationship between Judaism and psychotherapy, Rabbi Howard Cooper speaks of Freud's 'pre-eminence as the originator of the Jewish science, and art, of psychotherapy' (1988: xx). Whether or not we agree with Cooper's sentiments, there can be no doubt about the contribution to psychotherapy of Freud, who called himself the 'Godless Jew'.

Islam

As in the case of Judaism, Islam finds its pastoral guidelines in its sacred scriptures. For the Sunni Muslim, the largest group within Islam, their faith is expressed through conformity to the will of Allah as set out in the Shari'a, the body of texts that constitute the Islamic law. The most important of these are the Quran and the Sunna, a record of the deeds and sayings of the Prophet Muhammad (570–632):

> Matters of doctrine, worship, personal hygiene, family life, commerical affairs, and government are all treated in the Shari'a. It lays out a totalistic scheme for living as well as the elements of religion. In principle, therefore, believers who conform to its dictates both achieve merit in eternity and remove obstacles to their prosperity in this world. Within such a system pastoral care is embedded in the prescribed duties incumbent upon all Muslims.
>
> (Gaffney 1990: 596)

Gaffney also points out that, strictly speaking, while Islam rejects the notion of a clergy, a distinctively pastoral authority has been bestowed upon certain scholars because of their superior knowledge of the law. As well as presiding at rituals and preaching, they also admonmish, issue opinions and respond to situations of particular perplexity or distress.

There is a further interesting parallel between Judaism and Islam. We have already noted that in both religions, their traditional pastoral practice is based on conformity with the law. However, just as

Judaism has given birth to the gentler, more person-centred, Hasidic approach to the care of persons, Islam too has seen a reaction against its more legalistic formulations. Developing in Iraq and Iran between the eighth and thirteenth centuries, Sufism is a mystical strand within Islam which advocates asceticism and meditation as a means of achieving mystical union with the Divine. A contemporary Westernized expression of this is found in the Sufi Order of the West founded by Hazrat Inayat Khan (1882–1927). In a collection of papers published posthumously, *Spiritual Dimensions of Psychology* (1989), he explored the role of the mind in the spiritual life. This work has been continued by his son, Pir Vilayat Inayat Khan. In *Counselling and Therapy: The Spiritual Dimension* (1993), he attempts to bring together aspects of Eastern spirituality with the contemporary Western concern for personal growth. The aim is to use techniques of meditation in order to gain greater self-awareness and a higher perspective on the nature of interpersonal relationships. Commenting on a case involving a man, his wife and 'the other woman', he writes:

> The therapist's only way of helping them is to get them to get into a very high state of consciousness and see the whole thing: the meaning of their lives and what life is doing to them in terms of their enfoldment. They can be helped to realize that situations on earth will never be perfect – in fact they are sometimes really disastrous – but that they can handle things beautifully.
>
> (Khan 1993: 83)

This approach claims to introduce spirituality into counselling and therapy. Perhaps it would be truer to say that it is psychological insights that are brought to bear upon this particular form of spiritual direction. But, as I shall later point out, there is, in the Christian tradition, a similar convoluted relationship between the ancient art of spiritual direction and modern psychology. What we need to become aware of is the subtlety of their interrelationship in the search for an authentic humanity.

Before departing from this brief look at Islam, it is perhaps worth noting one aspect of Sufism which has recently come to prominence. Originating in the Middle East around 2500BC, the Enneagram was rediscovered and developed by certain Sufi orders in the fourteenth and fifteenth centuries. Essentially a system of classifying people according to nine personality types, it was made known in the West by George Ivanovich Gurdijeff, born in the Caucasus during the 1870s and a student of Sufi, Indian and Christian mysticism.

The Enneagram found its way into the human potential movement of the 1960s through the work of Oscar Ichazo. In the early 1970s several American Jesuit priests learned the material at the Esalen Institute and began to adapt it to meet their counselling needs with seminarians and lay people. It is now used extensively as a tool by some Western therapists working in a religious context.

Hinduism

A major barrier to transcultural dialogue is to try to understand one culture in terms of the thought categories of one's own. Nowhere is this more true than in comparing the psychologies and psychotherapies of East and West. Anderson writes:

> The East, believing in no *psyche*, until lately has had no psychology as such, holding its psychology in the form of religions, which were interested in therapeutic methods leading to enlightenment. In the modern West questions of health and salvation have been sharply distinguished and assigned to different cultural spheres (Science and religion).
>
> (Anderson 1990: 999)

Among the traditional features of Hindu culture and religion have been the caste system, a belief in reincarnation and the idea of *karma* or moral causation. While Western psychotherapies tend to help individuals assert their independence in relation to this world, Eastern psychologies require the renunciation of individuality. The concept of salvation or *moksha* signifies emancipation from the bonds of present existence. In this process the *guru* or spiritual master has a special role. Through meditation or yoga, the *guru* enables the disciple to give up illusions about the realities of this world. The culture is essentially patriarchal, women attaining *moksha* as they are reborn as males.

In a paper on 'Pastoral Counselling in the Hindu Cultural Context', given at the Fourth International Congress on Pastoral Care and Counselling, Padmasani Gallup (1992) takes the view that counselling should seek to reinforce rather than undermine Hindu cultural values. She describes a case of a Hindu woman, Kala, the mother of two young children, who was abused both physically and emotionally by her husband, Kumar, an educated government employee. Overindulged by both parents, Kumar's behaviour, while inexcusable, was understandable in terms of cultural norms which subserved the psychosocial development of the Hindu male. In counselling Kala, Gallup saw the task in rather different terms from those that might be anticipated in a Western psychotherapeutic approach. Since the status of the Hindu woman who is divorced or separated is intolerable, counselling needs to encourage Kala to win her husband over to a more responsible and thoughtful way of relating to her and the children:

> Counselling is directed towards achieving the ideal wholeness of male-female partnership as visioned in the Athanareesvara union of Siva and Parvathi, gods of Hindu Saivaism. It is sometimes referred to as the union of Sivam and Sakti = goodness and power. In this search for wholeness the whole family, aunts, uncles, cousins, etc., could be involved.
>
> (Gallup 1992: 70)

This case illustrates the sensitivity to cultural values of an Indian woman highly trained in the skills of North American pastoral counselling. It is a reminder that in all counselling, cultural values and belief systems need to be taken seriously.

Buddhism

Whether or not Buddhism may be considered a religion is a matter of definition. It is, however, clearly a spiritual philosophy. Founded on the life and teaching of Siddhartha Gotama, who lived in Northern India some five hundred years before Jesus Christ, it eschews the worship of any deity. Yet with its sacred writings, its distinctive world view, its monastic orders, its many rituals and its meditative practices, Buddhism in its different forms displays many of the characteristics of a religious faith. The son of a prince, Siddhartha Gotama renounced the privileges of his birth to become a wandering ascetic in search of a higher truth. When the ascetic way proved to be fruitless he turned to meditation, attaining an enlightenment that caused him to be called the Buddha or Enlightened One. After his Enlightenment, the Buddha taught his followers 'the Middle way' which rejected both sensual indulgence and ascetic austerity.

For the Buddhist the problem is not sin but suffering which results not from guilt as understood by Christians but simply as part of the 'givenness' of life. If we are not to be held in the grip of suffering we must eliminate desire and acquire complete detachment. It is through meditation that this becomes possible. In an article on 'Buddhism and Counselling', Tony Martin describes meditation as 'the creation of an inner space in which one learns to observe the arising and passing away alike of joy and sadness, love and hate, elation and depression' (1985: 23).

Buddhist meditation has also been described in a broadcast talk by Derek Wright:

> The object of meditation is to make what is for most people a fitful, brief, partial, incidental and unnoticed event of awareness into something strong, clear and continuous. Now this is not at all the same as self-consciousness (as that is ordinarily understood) for when we're self-conscious we're not only observing ourselves but also evaluating ourselves in the light of what others may think; nor is it like self-examination in the sense in which Christians ordinarily understand the term, for in self-examination you're measuring yourself up against some moral yardstick and you're ticking yourself off. Nor is it like the contemplative prayer of the mystic, for the contemplative mystic is aware of God or the clear light of the void and so on, whereas in this kind of meditation it is your own physical and mental processes you are aware of. Nor is it very much like what goes in in psychotherapy, where what you are doing most of the time is remembering things and thinking about them. It is, to repeat, the cultivation of a clear, non-interfering, bare awareness of what is going on inside oneself.
>
> (Wright 1970)

Buddhist meditation, this cultivation of a clear awareness of what is going on inside onself, can be of therapeutic value. In a paper on 'Buddhism and Psychotherapy', Ian Wray writes:

> What of Buddhist practices such as meditation? Can these be of use to the person suffering from neurosis, even if he is a long way from attaining *dhyana*? [Note: Elsewhere Wray defines *dhyana* as referring to various states of mind characterized by concentration, tranquillity and positive emotion. DL] The straightforward answer is that they can, in neurotic people (and even psychotic people) have gained great value from meditation without first attaining *dhyana* . . . They see through their neuroses and what is maintaining them. The 'mindfulness of breathing' is a meditation which is intended for the cultivation of 'mindfulness', a crucial faculty according to Buddhism, which one can perhaps paraphrase as 'awareness'. The meditation itself, apart from cultivating awareness, is also effective in bringing tranquillity and clarity to the mind, and increasing a person's energy.
>
> (Wray 1986: 168)

We can also discern the importance of self-awareness in the work of a clinical psychologist who happens to be a Buddhist in the Japanese Soto Zen tradition. Neil Rothwell writes of the anxieties experienced by therapists themselves in the course of counselling:

If the therapist has been in the habit of using more structured therapies, the discomfort can be acute, as the focus of attention has previously been 'outward' to the techniques and their implementation rather than 'inward' to his or her inner experience. Presumably these discomforts have been present all the time but awareness of them has been blocked by focusing predominantly on the technique. This seems a shaky foundation on which to build therapy. The effect of becoming aware of these feelings, however, is that they gradually lose power and the therapist is able to let go of them. The result is that the therapist is less afraid to give of himself or herself, and this act of giving naturally allows positive personal qualities to show themselves.

(Rothwell 1993: 13)

Rothwell points to a fact of wider significance for all therapists: namely, that there is the need for all who counsel others to be aware of their own thoughts, feelings and values. This is especially important for those who offer help within the pastoral and spiritual context where the boundary between explicit and implicit beliefs and values may be hazy. Perhaps it is no less important for those who think that they bring *no* explicitly religious ideas to their counselling because sometimes the therapist's implicit values and unacknowledged feelings can be insidious in their effects on the client. For this reason competent, regular supervision is as important in this context as in any other.

At the beginning of this chapter, we examined the nature of counselling within the Christian Church and, in this section, we have explored the relationship between belief and therapy in relation to four important world religions. However, this does not exhaust the possibilities of counselling in a spiritual context. So having moved from 'church' to 'religion' we now explore the meaning of 'spirituality' and its relationship to counselling.

COUNSELLING AND THE SPIRITUAL JOURNEY

It is a paradox of the late twentieth century that when institutional religion appears to be in decline, there is a burgeoning interest in spirituality. Yet, while there is now much talk about spirituality, there is little agreement about what is meant by the word. The 'Spirituality' sections of religious bookshops are larger than ever, selling books describing every variety of spirituality from Ignatian to New Age. Indeed, many bookshops now *specialize* in New Age and what were once thought to be esoteric forms of spirituality.

Within the Christian Church there is a long tradition of spiritual direction. The Desert Fathers of the fourth and fifth centuries in Egypt and Syria had their disciples who came seeking advice and guidance. In the sixth century Gregory the Great, in his *Pastoral Care* (Oden 1984), laid the foundations of pastoral ministry as the care of souls. In the Celtic tradition of the same era, the time of Patrick and Columba, we encounter the 'soul-friend' who, according to Kenneth Leech (1977: 40), antedates Christianity, every Celtic chief having his counsellor or druid at court. Thereafter the spread of monasticism gave rise to a wide variety of different kinds of spiritual direction. An important figure in the post-Reformation Catholic Church, whose work is increasingly valued today in both Catholic and Protestant circles, is Ignatius of Loyola. Ignatian spirituality emphasises the place of imagination in an approach to meditation which should lead to greater self-knowledge. Attempts have been made to integrate the Ignatian *Spiritual Exercises* with modern psychotherapies, of which one example is the 'Christotherapy' of B. J. Tyrell (1982) who maintains that psychotherapy and spiritual direction cannot be separated. While primarily intended for Christians who wish to pursue growth and healing in an explicitly Christ-centred context, it is held that Christ is present, and at work at least anonymously, in all healing and growth. The aims of Christotherapy are based upon the four notional 'weeks' of the Ignatian schema with their emphasis on *reforming, conforming, confirming* and *transforming* (Benner 1988: 160).

Spiritual direction is not only a feature of Roman Catholic Church life. There is a long and lively tradition of spiritual direction with Anglicanism (Thornton 1956, 1984). Within the Reformed tradition, there is a new interest in the spiritual experiences of men and women. Howard Rice in his *Reformed Spirituality* (1991) has uncovered another side of Calvin from the one portrayed by the arid scholasticism of some Calvinists. This Calvin emphasized the primacy of human experience over theory, was aware of the importance of private prayer, of quietness before God and the meditative reading of the Bible, and recommended the keeping of a journal.

Pastoral counselling and spiritual direction

There are obvious similarities between pastoral counselling and
spiritual direction. Both are helping or supportive relationships
offered in a faith context and both may take place in either a one-
to-one or a group setting. There are differences between them but
they are related to one another. Martin Thornton, a leading Anglican authority on spiritual direction, writes:

> Nevertheless, despite these plain differences of approach, an
> interplay between counseling and direction is both possible and
> desirable: the most gifted of the faithful could still benefit from
> counsel, and, if only as a by-product of its primary object, prayer
> can be therapeutic. Or perhaps direction could be regarded as
> the consummation and conclusion of counseling. Christian living,
> based on the gospel and assisted by subsidiary sciences, is a
> composite whole, with prayer as the synthesizing catalyst. In
> competent pastoral care, it is important to understand the parts
> which make up the whole.
>
> (Thornton 1990: 1210)

If, then, we are to regard pastoral counselling and spiritual direction as two parts of the totality of the Church's ministry of pastoral
care, how are the parts to be related to one another? Within the
ranks of the spiritual directors there is a spectrum of opinion on this
matter. Indeed, in *Soul Friend*, Kenneth Leech takes the view that
the two parts must be quite clearly distinguished (1977: 100). First,
while counselling is concerned with states of emotional distress, the
ministry of spiritual direction is more important when there are no
particular crises. Earlier, R. S. Lee, discussing the difference between
counselling and confession, wrote:

> In confession, it is the spiritually and psychologically mature
> penitent who is most able to gain from it. The disintegrated and
> mal-developed are more likely to become fixed in their weakness.
>
> (Lee 1968: 116)

For Leech, while there is a degree of overlap, the priest is a
spiritual director and not a therapist, and spiritual direction is not
the same as therapy. Second, while counselling is clinic-based or
office-based, spiritual direction is firmly located within the sacramental and liturgical life of the Body of Christ. Third, Leech felt that
in pastoral counselling, there was too much emphasis on helping
individuals to adjust to society while the task of Christian ministry
was to enable individuals to act corporately in the transformation

of society. Elsewhere (1986), Leech has drawn attention to the connection between Anglican spirituality and some remarkable pastoral ministries in areas of social deprivation.

While Leech's distinctions between pastoral counselling and spiritual direction are clear and well-defined, they are held rather less starkly by more recent writers. Thus, there are other spiritual directors who, while maintaining the distinction, also wish to be more explicit about the interrelationship of these two components of pastoral care. Gerald May is a psychiatrist who is also director for spiritual guidance at the Shalem Institute for Spiritual Formation in Washington, DC. In his *Care of Mind: Care of Spirit*, he writes:

> Yet it is obvious that all people entering spiritual direction have psychological concerns that are part of their spirituality. To attempt too strict a separation, to try to divorce mind from spirit, would be artificial and not at all helpful. We are human souls with body, mind and spirit all reflecting aspects of our unified being. To look to the spirit without addressing the mind is as absurd as caring for the mind without attending to physical health.
>
> (May 1992: 14)

May then proceeds to examine the differences between psychotherapy and spiritual direction in the light of *content* and *intent*. As far as content is concerned, while psychotherapy focuses more on mental and emotional dimensions, spiritual direction focuses more precisely in spiritual issues such as prayer life, religious experiences and relationship to God. To fail to keep these two dimensions separate, to label every experience a spiritual experience and every therapy a form of spiritual direction, usually means that any real attention to spiritual matters is lost in the undertaking. The main intent of psychotherapy is normally to strengthen the individual's autonomy and to enable the satisfaction of needs and desires. Spiritual direction, in enabling self-surrender to the discerned will of God, may run counter to the apparent cultural values of psychotherapy.

Again, when Leech argued that spiritual direction was located within the community of faith rather than in the office or clinic, he paid tribute to the views of Robert Lambourne (see page 36) but felt that the latter was a voice crying in the wilderness. It could be argued that Leech did not foresee Lambourne's subsequent influence. According to Alastair Campbell, 'Lambourne remains, despite his premature death, a major influence on pastoral studies in Britain' (1990: 630). And in the United States there are signs of the rediscovery of pastoral counselling as a ministry of the Church (Patton: 1983).

Finally, Leech criticized the pastoral counselling movement for its excessive focus on the problems of individuals with its ethos of adjustment rather than transformation. It has to be admitted that this is a fair criticism of what has been, and still is, a weakness of much counselling, whether in the pastoral or indeed any other context. It must be recognized, however, that sometimes in counselling, when encountering a person in deep distress about a situation which cannot be changed, the primary aim of the counsellor may well be to sustain a client or parishioner in adversity and to adjust to new circumstances. And that is not the whole story. There is also a fresh awareness of the social and political context of pastoral counselling. In *Liberating God* (1983), Peter Selby maintains that pastoral care and political involvement are mutually dependent. He holds in creative tension the outward and inward journeys. On the one hand those whose initial commitment was to social and political change have been driven inwards, their secular theologies lying under the debris of shattered political dreams; on the other there are those whose pastoral concern has led them into the political struggle, arguing that Martin Luther King did not lead a movement for the civil rights of his people on any other ground than pastoral concern (1983: 6).

The relationship between pastoral counselling and spiritual direction has an interesting parallel to the one we explored earlier in this chapter between pastoral counselling and so-called Christian counselling, the former arising out of the catholic tradition of the Church and the latter from the evangelical. It points to the way in which religious belief cannot be separated from the nature and content of the helping relationship. It arises in a particularly acute form in counselling in the pastoral and spiritual context and must therefore be addressed again in Chapter Four which deals with issues specific to the context. What we must ask is whether the facing of issues which are inevitably quite explicit in this context does not reveal their implicit presence in other contexts; to this issue we shall also return.

Counselling and the search for meaning

The contemporary interest in spirituality is not confined to the Christian church. Coincidental with the writing of these paragraphs, there appeared in *The Scotsman Weekend*, an article by Leila Farrah (1993) comparing three contrasting retreat centres in Scotland. These were a Catholic Benedictine monastry at Pluscarden, the Buddhist Samye Ling Tibetan Centre in the Borders, and the New Age Centre of Light in the Highlands. Farrah's comparison of the three centres is fascinating in itself, with only the New Age Centre claiming to offer some kind of therapy. 'Using language and imagery which would send a materialist screeching from the premises,' the therapists attempted to help the author work through a recent traumatic experience in her personal life. While Farrah found the therapists personally supportive, she also found some aspects of the guidance offered 'a tad superfluous' and thought that people not in sympathy with New Age ideas would find the set-up bizarre and Bohemian. What is perhaps more significant than the content of the article is the fact that it was published in a prominent position in one of Scotland's quality newspapers. At a time when contemporary culture is increasingly being shaped by rapid technological development, and mainsteam religion appears in decline, there is a renewed interest in spirituality.

In this chapter I have shown the centrality of the helping relationship within all the major religions of the world. I have also noted the growth of the practice of counselling as part of the life of very different traditions within the Christian Church, and the surprising interest in many diverse kinds of spirituality, both Christian and non-Christian, which exists alongside the apparent decline in institutional religion. Perhaps I need hardly also draw attention to the remarkable growth of the counselling movement itself over the past few years.

What does it all mean? Is there any connection between these various phenomena? Why do people get involved in counselling? Is the growth of the counselling movement related to the decline in institutional religion? Whatever function religion has in the lives of people, it does give a framework of meaning and value. In the absence of faith in established forms of religion, is it involvement in counselling that enables people to find an alternative framework? In using the term 'involvement in counselling', I deliberately include counsellor as well as client. The huge rise in the numbers of those training in counselling might indicate an attempt to find new purpose and meaning. There is, of course, one school of psychotherapy where 'man's search for meaning' is the dominant theme. Victor Frankl, another Jewish psychotherapist from Vienna, emphasized the 'will to meaning' as a basic human motivation over against Freud's 'will to pleasure' (1988). The ideas behind his 'Logotherapy', while conceived of earlier, were confirmed by his experiences in a Nazi concentration camp. Those who survived had something to live for. Frankl believed that it was a lack of a sense of meaning which lay behind some neuroses – the 'noogenic neuroses'. The task of therapy was to enable patients to find for themselves the meaning of their own existence. For Frankl, spirituality (along with freedom and responsibility), was one of the three constituents of human experience. Frankl makes a strong case for the exploration of meaning as part of the counselling process and his ideas have had obvious attractions and relevance for counselling in this context.

Frankl's concern was that in counselling the client or patient should find meaning. But what of the counsellor? Why *do* people become counsellors? I suspect that research would show that many people who become counsellors have themselves benefited from counselling. Having been accompanied on their own journey, and perhaps helped through a difficult time, they have experienced healing, grown in self-awareness and to their own surprise found themselves becoming a companion to others. This is particularly true of many self-help groups where the most effective helpers are the wounded healers who have experienced the same trauma and distress. The transition from being wounded to becoming healer is part of the journey of many counsellors. That journey may lie within one of the traditions of Christianity, or within another of the world's great religions, or it may take the form of a spirituality which is part of the quest for that which is most authentically human. Whatever the nature of their own journey, there can be few counsellors in any context who do not bring to their task both a world view and a personal agenda that transcends the simple application of technique. Perhaps in confronting this issue as a matter of necessity in this context, we shall throw some light on counselling in other contexts where the beliefs and values of the counsellor, while more implicit, may still be of significance for the counselling process.

· THREE ·

The practice of counselling in the pastoral and spiritual context

Before becoming a minister of the Lutheran Church in America, Richard Krebs, already a PhD in clinical psychology, had extensive experience of counselling. Looking forward to his parish work, he thought: 'I don't know how I will be as a preacher or administrator, but I am sure I will be a good pastoral counsellor.' Two years into his ministry, he wrote an article for the *Journal of Pastoral Care* called 'Why Pastors Should Not Be Counselors' (Krebs 1980), in which he set out what he considered to be the obstacles to exercising a long-term counselling ministry in a parish context. Some time later the same journal published a response to Krebs, 'Why Pastors *Should* be Counselors [of a Sort]' (Switzer 1983) by one of America's leading teachers of pastoral counselling. Taken together, these two articles help us to focus upon many of the important issues involved in the practice of counselling in a pastoral and spiritual context.

What happened to make Richard Krebs change his mind about the place of counselling in parish ministry? He listed four problems which he considered to be inherent in the situation and which must inevitably lead to failure. These were:

1 *The promise of cheap growth.* Parishioners come looking for quick solutions to their problems and are not usually prepared for the time-consuming and emotionally upsetting process that may be involved in personal growth. Krebs believed that this was a strain which should not be imposed on the relationship between pastor and parishioner.

2 *Transference.* The phenomenon of transference is inevitably present in any pastoral relationship and the pastor cannot assume the

role of anonymous, 'faceless' therapist necessary to resolve the transference.

3 *Role confusion.* It is impossible for the pastor to combine the role of therapist with that of preacher, teacher, liturgist, committee member, family friend and moral example. In such a situation confidentiality becomes impossible, to say nothing of the objectivity and client-centred focus which is necessary for successful therapy.

4 *Misplaced priorities.* Long-term counselling is time-consuming and detracts from the pastor's ability to carry out the more mundane tasks which he is expected to do and for which he is paid.

For all these reasons, pastors should not attempt to be psychotherapists in their own congregations. Their counselling role should be confined to evaluation, the provision of support and referral, and informal brief therapy:

> The training of pastors should not include a major emphasis on counselling *per se*, but should rather focus on listening skills, and the personality (or more properly the *person*) of the pastor. Being able to really listen to a parishioner and to respond to them with caring are *all* that a pastor needs to do.
>
> (Krebs 1980: 233)

In response, Switzer acknowledges elements of truth in Krebs' position but challenges it at certain points:

1 What does Krebs understand by counselling? He seems to envisage nothing between long-term, in-depth psychotherapy and brief, informal pastoral encounters. Switzer points out that between these two extremes there are a number of situations, for example in marriage counselling, which could comfortably be handled by suitable trained pastors in less then six to eight sessions.

2 As far as role confusion is concerned, that is a fact of parish life. Pastoral counselling, as one form of pastoral care, is merely one function, and a legitimate one, within the role of minister, as preacher, teacher, priest, administrator, etc.

3 While Krebs has to be heard on the issue of misplaced priorities, it applies equally to ministers who over-emphasize preaching or teaching to the extent that they neglected pastoral ministry and fail to make themselves available to those who need to see them for one or two counselling sessions.

4 On the matter of transference, Switzer is in radical disagreement with Krebs. Certainly, too few ministers are aware of this significant dynamic in their relationships with people. But (he writes):

I believe Krebs to be wrong when he says 'In order for the transference to be resolved, the therapist must be an anonymous, "faceless", individual (p. 230). Being the *imago incognito* is in fact conducive to the *establishment* of the transference neurosis, not its resolution. The resolution of each occasion of transference which takes place is accomplished by the therapist being known as the human being that he or she actually is . . . The minister is a living moving target for transference by many people when that minister is functioning as preacher, priest, teacher and even in short-term pastoral counseling . . . Since we ministers, as a result of our particular and unique relationships with persons, do receive emotions and fantasies and expectations which were originally learned earlier in relationship to others, a part of our competence is the ability to recognize this when it takes place and to respond to others with genuineness in the reality of the present.

(Switzer 1983: 31)

Switzer, therefore, sees a much more positive and necessary role for counselling in the context of parish ministry, believing that not only do parishioners not require referral to another professional, but that at times their minister is the very person they want and need to talk to and who can be their most effective helper.

The Krebs-Switzer debate, outlined above, is located within only one corner of what we have seen to be the wide canvas of counselling in a pastoral or spiritual context. Nevertheless, I believe that in this discussion, although narrowly focused on counselling in the context of parish ministry, there are allusions, either explicit or implicit, to fundamental issues that must be addressed when we consider the practice of counselling in the wider context. In this chapter I examine four main issues where pastoral counselling overlaps with counselling in other contexts, yet where there are aspects of each issue unique to the pastoral context. These are (a) issues related to confidentiality; (b) the question of appropriate boundaries especially in relation to sexuality in pastoral counselling; (c) the problem of payment for pastoral or spiritual help; and (d) matters relating to competence and supervision.

CONFIDENTIALITY

Krebs identifies confidentiality as a problem when counselling in a parish situation. Although he does not say why this should be so, not much imagination is needed to pinpoint the possible difficulties. If one member of a family is meeting the minister on a regular basis, other members of the family will probably be aware of the fact. Even the most non-committal response to well-intended (or even downright inquisitive) expressions of interest from relatives will say too much or is likely to be misinterpreted.

Why is confidentiality so important, not only in counselling, but in all relationships of a professional or helping nature? Two reasons, each corresponding to one of the two main types of ethical theory, have been given. Those who approach ethical dilemmas by looking at the probable results of actions, the *Consequentialists*, argue that the failure to observe confidentiality would result in it becoming impossible for doctor and patient, or lawyer and client, or minister and parishioner, or counsellor and client to work together. If confidentiality is not guaranteed, hurting people will not share their distress. The other main school of ethical theorists, the *Deontologists* (which comes from a word meaning 'duty'), justify confidentiality either by relating it to the duty of promise-keeping, if an implied or explicit promise has been made, or to the duty to respect the autonomy of persons who in this case would otherwise lose control over important information about themselves (Walters 1986: 112).

The presumption of confidentiality in a pastoral setting has deep historical roots. In *A History of the Cure of Souls* (1951), McNeill traces the history of the seal of confession. While Ambrose in the fourth century felt obligated to 'tell none but the Lord' the nature of offences revealed to him in private, McNeill found no specific evidence in Church law of insistence on secrecy before the middle of the ninth century. Around 1010 there are indications that a priest breaking the seal of the confessional was to be deposed (1951: 117). In later years there was some debate as to whether the seal should be inviolate, where the confession involved facts that would disqualify persons from marriage or clerics from ordination. Or, if a confessant declares his intention to kill his father or his king, could he claim the privilege of the seal? (1951: 147). The clear evidence is, however, that in all traditions of the Church, Protestant as well as Catholic, the confidentiality of the relationship between minister and parishioner has been held to be sacrosanct.

Medically qualified counsellors, in their professional relationships, have an even longer tradition of secrecy embodied in the Hippocratic Oath dating from the fifth century BC. This states:

Whatever, in connection with my professional practice, or not in connection with it, I see or hear, in the life of men, which

ought not to be spoken of abroad, I will not divulge, as reck-
oning that all such should be kept secret.

(Gillon 1985: 106)

While this is fine in theory, it is sometimes difficult to observe in
practice, particularly within the context of a modern teaching hospital. In the ward of such a hospital many people may be directly
involved in the care of the patients, medical and nursing staff,
physiotherapists, speech therapists, occupational therapists, social
workers and chaplains, as well as students on placement with all
these disciplines. It is obviously impractical for every professional
person who enters into conversation with a patient to obtain permission concerning exactly what information may be shared with
the rest of the extended team. This problem is acute precisely in
those medical teams that take a holistic approach to patients with
a concern for their social, emotional and spiritual well-being. Various
steps can be taken to alleviate the problem. At the very least, patients should be made aware that their cases may be discussed
within a wider team, but that within that wider group all personal
details are treated as confidential. Chaplains who function as part
of such teams must constantly distinguish between information
imparted to them which has nothing to do with patients' medical
condition, which must be kept confidential, and information which
may be relevant which they should seek permission from patients
to share. These decisions are often difficult but they are the kind of
professional decisions which are central to the practice of hospital
chaplaincy. The alternatives are for chaplains either to observe no
restrictions on what they share with other professionals (which is
ethically unacceptable) or to cease to function as part of the
therapeutic team (which is pastorally undesirable). In fact most of
the issues of confidentiality which surround pastoral care in the
hospital setting are usually resolved where there is trust and mutual
confidence between chaplains and senior ward staff. While these
relational qualities are as intangible as they are real, there is no
doubt that where they exist, patients benefit in the support they
receive from a mutually supportive team.

The ordained minister can look to the seal of the confessional,
and the medical doctor to the Hippocratic Oath, for historical prec-
edents in matters relating to confidentiality. The counsellor who is
neither minister nor doctor must seek other sources of guidance. In
many cases, those who counsel in the pastoral and spiritual context
are in the same position as those who counsel in the voluntary
sector; the observations made by Tyndall in another volume in this

series are applicable (Tyndall 1993: 51). The British Association for Counselling has drawn up a *Code of Ethics and Practice for Counsellors* (1992) in which considerable emphasis is given to confidentiality. What is evident is that while confidentiality is regarded as being of the utmost importance in counselling, it is not given the absolute status of the seal of confession:

> Exceptional circumstances may arise which give the counsellor good grounds for believing that the client will cause serious physical harm to others or themselves, or have harm caused to him/her. In such circumstances the client's consent to a change in the agreement about confidentiality should be sought whenever possible unless there are also good grounds for believing the client is no longer able to take responsibility for his or her actions. Whenever possible, the decision to break confidentiality agreed between a counsellor and client should be made only after consultation with a counselling supervisor or an experienced counsellor.
>
> (BAC 1992: 4.4)

Supervision must of necessity raise issues of confidentiality and here it is important that clients should know, wherever possible, that the counsellor discusses his or her work with someone more experienced. A further safeguard in supervision is to present case material anonymously so that it is not possible to identify the client.

Confidentiality as a legal issue

The BAC Code makes two further distinctions that are important for counselling in the pastoral and spiritual context. The first is the distinction between confidentiality as an ethical issue and confidentiality as a legal issue. The Code points out that:

> Generally speaking, there is no legal duty for a counsellor to give information spontaneously. Refusal to answer police questions is not an offence, though lying could be. In general terms, the only circumstances in which police can require an answer about a client, and when refusal to answer would be an offence, relate to the prevention of terrorism. It is good practice to ask police personnel to clarify their legal right to an answer before refusing to give one.
>
> (BAC 1992: B.5.1)

Are ministers and priests in a different legal position from counsellors who are not ordained? It is difficult to give a precise answer.

A distinction has been made in the United States between the Seal of Confession, Privileged Communication and Confidential Information. The Seal of Confession has been regarded as sacrosanct and there is no indication that it has ever been challenged in the law courts. 'Privileged Communication' is a category covering various professional relationships, and in some States clear criteria exist for identifying such communication. Yet because there is no federal law defining the 'religious privilege', each State has developed its own statutes leading to widely different practices (Dechant 1991: 65).

Scots law is no more definite on the subject. In *The Scottish Law of Evidence*, Wilkinson (1986) discusses various cases involving communication between the clergy and those accused of crimes. He quotes one authority which holds that any privilege is almost certainly that of the person who communicates with the ministers and not of the ministers themselves. There was also a problem of definition. Although it might be possible to define a member of the clergy, there is a certain arbitrariness in stopping short of a spiritual confidante such as (in one case) a jailer. Wilkinson concludes that 'the trend of the authorities, although inconclusive, is perhaps towards affirming the privilege' (Wilkinson 1986: 106).

Surely what is important is that despite any ambiguities in the legal position, the utmost care should be taken to protect the confidentiality of pastoral relationships with clients and parishioners.

Confidentiality and the use of counselling skills

The second distinction the BAC Code identifies is that between counsellors and those who use counselling skills as part of another professional role. It could be argued that much of the counselling undertaken in the pastoral and spiritual context falls within this category, for example, by ministers as they go about their normal pastoral duties. The burden of advice given by the BAC Code is that agreements made about confidentiality should be consistent with any written code(s) governing the functional role of the user of the counselling skills. Until recently this might have seemed irrelevant advice as far as most Churches were concerned, since there were few, if any, such written codes. This situation is changing. In 1990 the Diocese of Bristol produced a document *Toward a Code of Practice for Pastoral Care by the Clergy*, which focuses on aspects of good pastoral practice such as awareness of the pastor's own needs, the necessity of supervision and spiritual direction, and the importance of confidentiality and record-keeping. In similar vein, both the

Methodist Church in Britain (1991) and the Church of Scotland (1993a) are beginning to produce codes of professional conduct for their ministers.

BOUNDARIES

There are a number of issues which, while they are common to counselling in other contexts, occur with their own special nuances in the pastoral context. I have already drawn attention to the great diversity of the forms of pastoral counselling. It is true that a minister in a parish, a hospital chaplain and a counsellor working in a pastoral centre all experience boundary problems, but they are not the same. In many ways the problems of the minister in a local congregation are the most acute. While Krebs and Switzer give different weight to the matter of role-confusion in a parish setting, neither denies that a problem exists. It *is* difficult to preach on Sunday and then to counsel a member of that congregation on Monday, although if there is a lack of congruence between the preaching role and the pastoral role, it might be worth asking which of them provides the true picture of the minister's beliefs and values. A minister whose preaching consistently offers a religion of high ideals, creating feelings of guilt among the congregation for their failure to attain them, is not likely to be approached by people whose self-esteem is already low. Again, it is not easy, and sometimes quite impossible, to enter into a counselling relationship with someone with whom one has openly disagreed in a church meeting. Furthermore, in the parish context, where much counselling begins within the informal structures of pastoral care, it can be difficult to move to the more formal contracts required for successful counselling. For one thing, such formalities as time-bound meetings may not be expected by the parishioner; for another, there already exists a possibly deeper kind of implicit pastoral contract between minister and congregation: that a minister is constantly available for pastoral care, day and night – a contract which itself needs re-examining in many cases.

Institutional chaplains have boundary problems of a different kind. Working in situations that are much more interdisciplinary than the local congregation, there can be, from time to time, a problem in professional boundaries, for example, when a patient wants to talk about a personal problem. Sometimes a chaplain becomes involved with a patient not by virtue of being a minister or priest but simply by being at a bedside at the time when the patient wants to talk.

Occasionally a decision has to be made whether to continue with a conversation once begun or to refer the patient to a colleague in another department. Where staff in different departments trust the integrity and competence of their colleagues, the supportive network created can influence for good the morale of the whole institution. If, however, one profession believes it has a monopoly of counselling skills, petty rivalries can be quite destructive. I return to the issue of interprofessional co-operation in Chapter Five.

Theoretically, counsellors based in a centre should not experience the same type of boundary problems, since their role is quite clearly ' defined as a counselling one. Even in large cities, however, it is possible for clients to encounter their counsellors in other contexts. There are, however, other boundary issues encountered by all engaged in helping relationships.

Pastoral counselling and sexuality

A matter which has come increasingly within the public domain is that of sexual relationships between therapists and their clients. The definitive study has been Rutter's *Sex in the Forbidden Zone* (1989) in which he explores the growing evidence of sexual relationships between doctors and patients, lawyers and clients, lecturers and students, clergy and parishioners. Rutter is a psychiatrist and his interest in this issue was stimulated when a woman patient made sexual advances to him at a time in his life when he was himself emotionally vulnerable. In the event, he had the self-awareness required to defuse the situation, but reflection upon what had happened led him to begin an investigation into the problem. As news of his interest became known, stories of widespread abuse throughout all the professions began to accumulate. In the great majority (ninety-six per cent) of situations reported, men were in positions of authority. Rutter's analysis of why these situations come about is perceptive and illuminating. Working within an essentially Jungian perspective, he traces the problem to the existence of wounds deep within the psyche of both therapist and client:

> For both the man in power and his protégé, strong issues of self hang in the balance in the forbidden zone. A man's tendency to form sexual fantasy in the forbidden zone is an expression of his search for the aliveness of his own self . . . On the other hand, most women who have had exploitative sexual relationships experience a deep wound to their most inner, sacred sense of self. This psychological injury – often felt as the death

of hope itself – remains the greatest casualty of sex in the forbidden zone.

(Rutter 1989: 51)

Psychodynamically the transgression of sexual boundaries can be understood in terms of the transference which is part of all helping relationships, whether it is recognized or not. A patient trying to seduce a therapist may be repeating past injuries but is also probably searching for a response that will discourage the repetition. The therapist has the power either to re-injure his or her patients or to relate to them in a way that will free them from the wounds of the past.

Irrespective of the psychological roots of this phenomenon, there is widespread agreement about the degree of psychological damage caused, and that the practice is therefore unethical. The fact that so many women accept sexual advances from a therapist or mentor does not justify these liaisons, because in such situations the woman is always under some duress to comply. Even situations where the relationship is initiated by the woman provide no excuse for a therapist to take advantage of the client or a minister of a parishioner because 'a victim cannot consent to her own exploitation' (Rutter 1989: 265).

Yet Rutter also points to the therapeutic potential that comes through recognizing the erotic dimension which can be integral to many counselling relationships and responding to that reality with self-restraint:

> Because so many women have been previously injured by the uncontained sexuality of men who have had power over them, the potential healing power of restraint is enormous. Not only is the woman made safe from being exploited by this particular man, but the moment kindles the promise that she can be valued as a woman entirely apart from her sexual value to other men. In these moments life takes a new turn, and injury from the past as well as hopelessness about the future can be healed.

(Rutter 1989: 250)

To what extent is sexual exploitation a problem in counselling in a pastoral or spiritual context? In most denominations, even in those where women are ordained to the ministry, most ministers of local congregations are men. On the other hand most of the counsellors in church-related counselling centres are women. Therefore, if Rutter's statistics are correct, the problem is more likely to exist in the parish than in the counselling centre, though it is obviously difficult to measure its extent. One of the first American books on the subject was *The Problem Clergymen Don't Talk About* (Rassieur 1976). But it is being talked about more and more. The discussion document produced by the Methodist Church in Britain, *Some Elements of Pastoral Practice* (1991), is mainly concerned with the issues relating to intimacy and appropriate boundaries in pastoral relationships. This is a sensitively written document which is fully alive to the problems, not the least of these being that most pastoral conversations take place in people's homes, sometimes at a time of distress. Helpful guidelines of a practical nature are given, drawing attention to such matters as place and time and the presence nearby of other people.

THE COST OF COUNSELLING

One of the problems Krebs identified about counselling in a parish setting was the 'promise of cheap growth'. He was thinking particularly of the belief held by some parishioners that the minister might provide a simple solution to their problems at a cost of little personal pain or self-examination. His thinking here has overtones of the 'cheap grace' condemned by Dietriech Bonhoeffer in *The Cost of Discipleship* (1959):

> Cheap grace is the deadly enemy of the Church . . . Cheap grace means the justification of sin without the justification of the sinner . . . Cheap grace is the preaching of forgiveness without requiring repentance, baptism without church discipline, Communion without confession, absolution without personal confession.

> Costly grace is the Gospel which must be *sought* again and again, the gift which must be *asked* for, the door at which a man must *knock*.
>
> (Bonhoeffer 1959: 35–7)

Those unfamiliar with Bonhoeffer's theology might be forgiven for thinking it was based on something less than a Gospel of unconditional grace. But this would be to misunderstand him. For Bonhoeffer, as for Luther before him, the primacy of God's grace was the foundation upon which their whole theological position rested. For both, that grace was freely available to men and women because the cost had been paid by Jesus Christ on the cross. Yet

Bonhoeffer believed that the basic thrust of Luther's thought had come to be misunderstood:

> The outcome of the Reformation was the victory, not of Luther's perception of grace in all its purity and costliness, but of the vigilant religious instinct of man for the place where grace is to be obtained at the cheapest price. All that was needed was a subtle and almost imperceptible change of emphasis and the damage was done . . . Costly grace was turned into cheap grace without discipleship.
>
> (Bonhoeffer 1959: 41)

In counselling, cheap grace without discipleship may manifest itself through the idea that there can be cheap growth without some kind of personal commitment. While the issue of payment in other contexts has been addressed from practical and psychological perspectives, I am suggesting that in the pastoral and spiritual context (and perhaps in these other contexts too) there might also be a theological dimension.

Practical considerations are particularly important in voluntary counselling organizations (Tyndall 1993: 64). As a church representative on the Board of Management of a secular counselling agency, I recall the agonized discussion that took place when it was proposed that clients should be invited to make a financial contribution to bridge the gap between increasing costs and a decreasing local authority grant. Should it be a fee or a voluntary contribution? How much should be suggested? How should the matter be raised? Should this be left to counsellors or would a discreet notice, placed in the consulting-room together with some empty envelopes, suffice? Did not the whole idea of a financial contribution run counter to the ethos of the organization? I have also been involved in setting-up a pastoral counselling centre when it was evident from the beginning that fees would need to be charged to meet the running costs.

North Americans are much more up-front about such matters and the unanimous assumption in all the literature is that a fee will be charged for counselling. Ross (1990) identifies two main approaches to setting fees. With a **standard fee** policy everyone is charged the same amount. This has the advantage of simplicity and, provided the fee is high enough, there is no need for additional funding. It makes no provision, however, for those who cannot pay the full amount. A more common method of determining a counsellee's fee is that of the **sliding scale** where clients are asked to pay according to means. For this method to be effective, the

average fee paid must equal the cost of providing the service. This
has been called 'The "Robin Hood" Policy' (Hinkle 1977) because
those who can pay more to subsidize the less well-off. Hinkle identifies some practical problems. It is a dubious way of providing the
on-going funding to ensure continuity of service. Further, those
who pay at the top end of the scale, while wishing to have religiously orientated counselling, may resent being compelled to subsidize others. Finally, this latter group may then find that what they
are paying brings them within the price range of the professional
psychotherapists, and the policy may become self-defeating. Hinkle
favours a policy of having a fixed fee, which covers all the costs of
the centre, together with a financial aid fund to help the less well-
off, and that a centre should function within the limits of this fund.

However, there are considerations other than the merely practical
to be considered. Ross (1990) begins his article on 'Fees in Pastoral
Counseling' by addressing the psychological dimension with a quotation from Karl Menninger to the effect that counselling:

> must involve a sacrifice, otherwise it becomes a matter of in-
> difference in the patient's life. It is deeply rooted in the human
> mind that what is cheap is of little value and what is dear is
> valuable.
>
> (Menninger 1958: 35)

It is argued that without sacrifice, clients fail to become partners
in the counselling process. With no commitment, they may termi-
nate too soon, or feel guilt about taking up too much of the counsellor's time. Conversely:

> Open and direct discussion of fees can prove fruitful on a thera-
> peutic level. For clients, fees are often a significant therapeutic
> concern involving self-esteem, motivation and commitment.
>
> (Young 1989: 271)

In the light of this discussion we can return to Krebs' thesis that
long-term, in-depth counselling in a parish context is not viable. I
suspect that Krebs is essentially right. Certainly no minister of a
local congregation could charge one of his own members a fee for
pastoral counselling. Those who might benefit most are often those
who least wish to bother the minister, while those who might be
most eager to enter into long-term counselling arrangements are
those who should not do so, for all the other reasons Krebs suggests.
This does not mean that ministers with training and aptitude should
not exercise this kind of ministry, nor that people who wish to be
counselled by a minister should not have this facility available to

them. Perhaps this needs to be organized on a wider geographical basis (as it surely is in many places). Then ministers can refer difficult situations which cannot easily be dealt with in the context of the local congregation to another minister known to be adequately trained in counselling. Either within the setting of a counselling centre, or within the context of private practice, pastoral counselling can be offered by qualified ministers or lay people and the fee question may then be dealt with openly, free from the complications of long-term counselling in the local parish. In the pastoral context it is important that the fee question be dealt with openly. The issues of self-esteem, motivation and commitment which were identified above are not simply psychological issues. In this context they are also issues of spiritual importance. In Chapter Four I argue that the very fact the counselling takes place in a context labelled 'pastoral' or 'spiritual' inevitably introduces a dimension of meaning and value with implications for the process of counselling itself.

With a system of cross-referral in place there is no reason why parish clergy should not continue their ministries of pastoral care using their counselling skills, which may be quite considerable. Each type of ministry has its own value, with one proviso. Long-term counselling outside the parish, whether by clergy or lay people, and short-term counselling within the parish, must both be underwritten by competent supervision. It is to this matter, another concern held in common with all other types of counselling, that I now turn.

SUPERVISION IN THE PASTORAL CONTEXT

While the concept of supervision is a comparatively new one in pastoral care and counselling, the fact of superintendence is not. Bishops, presbyteries and other hierarchical church structures have always had a responsibility for overseeing the administration of church affairs as well as the doctrine and morals of those who hold office. But superintendence is not the same as supervision. Supervision is certainly concerned with ensuring standards of competence. In the context of counselling and pastoral ministry, however, it is also concerned with enabling the personal and professional growth of the person being supervised. It is interesting to note that while Krebs must have received a great deal of supervision in his training and work as a clinical psychologist, this is not mentioned as an option for ministers.

The development of supervision parallels the growth of the counselling movement itself, particularly within social work and in psychotherapy. Publications coming from within these disciplines, for example by Kadushin (1985) and by Ekstein and Wallerstein (1972) have been influential in shaping the theory and practice of supervision, not only in these professions but in the many different contexts in which counselling takes place, including the pastoral.

In pastoral care and counselling, the theory and practice of supervision has been greatly influenced by the highly developed system for the training and accreditation of supervisors which has been a feature of the North American clinical pastoral education movement. A growing body of literature has been produced such as the Chicago-based *Journal of Supervision and Training in Ministry*, which has appeared annually since 1978. Until recently, virtually all the British literature on supervision emanated from secular sources, and most of the literature on pastoral supervision has been American. *Helping the Helpers: Supervision and Pastoral Care* (Foskett and Lyall 1988) was an attempt to address issues of pastoral supervision in a British context.

A seminal paper on pastoral supervision was one written in 1966 by Thomas Klink, one time chaplain at the Menninger Foundation in Topeka, Kansas. His paper introduces key concepts into the discipline and is often drawn upon. It was the subject of a symposium published in 1989 in the *Journal of Supervision and Training in Ministry*. I draw here myself on Klink's definition and use it as a basis for exploring some issues in our own context. For Klink:

i)   Supervision is a unique and identifiable educational procedure;
ii) it requires as supervisor one who is both engaged in the practice of his profession and duly qualified to supervise;
iii) it assumes as student a candidate seeking fuller qualification in the practice of his (intended) profession;
iv) it requires for its setting an institution within whose activities there are functional roles in which student and supervisor can negotiate a 'contract for learning';
v)   the roles of both supervisor and student must be appropriate to their particular professional identity (in this case the Christian ministry);
vi) lastly, supervision requires for its environment a wider community of professional peers associated in a common task.

(Klink 1966: 176)

While this definition grew out of a situation where the implicit assumption was that the supervisees were in preparation for 'the Christian ministry', it also helps us to focus on issues which are important for the supervision of everyone who is counselling in a pastoral or spiritual context.

A unique and identifiable educational procedure

Supervision is about education, and therefore about the enabling of learning. Unfortunately there are still those who see education in terms of the communication of factual knowledge from one person to another; and there are those who embark on a course in counselling expecting to be taught appropriate skills. To be sure, there is a body of knowledge to be acquired and there are skills to be learned. But if the acquisition of knowledge and the development of skills are necessary in the making of counsellors and pastors, they are certainly not sufficient. The main instrument employed by both the counsellor and the pastor is the self and his or her own ability to form relationships with other people. It is therefore necessary to develop an awareness of how that instrument functions. Supervision is about personal learning, and inevitably supervision will draw attention to how the counsellor or pastor functions as a person in what is intended to be a helping relationship.

A helpful concept introduced by Klink into the vocabulary of supervision is that of the 'cross-grained experience':

> There are a number of significant incidents in the student's experience which relate more to his style of response than to his intellectual categories. In fact many of the changes sought in training are changes in ways of acting rather than in ways of thinking.
>
> (Klink 1966: 191)

For example, a former nurse became a candidate for the ministry. During her pastoral care placement in a hospital, her natural tendency was to want to *do* things for patients. It 'went against the grain' for her to sit back and let others serve the patient in practical ways. The supervisory task in this instance was to enable her to *be* with patients and to allow her to be comfortable in a different kind of helping relationship.

To describe supervision as personal learning can lead to a confusion between supervision and counselling itself. Yet, while similar, they are not the same. In counselling, the focus is on the personal needs of the counsellee; in supervision, the focus is upon the 'professional' mode of functioning of the counsellor. Personal issues are only allowed to intrude to the extent that they affect that mode of functioning. These personal issues may be addressed in supervision if this can be done without impinging too much on the process of supervision. If these issues are deep-seated, the accepted wisdom is that the counsellor should seek his or her own counselling outside the supervisory relationship. There are usually problems when people receiving long-term counselling have other significant relationships with their counsellors (including supervision) and to that extent Krebs was right to warn of the dangers of such counselling in a parish setting. Neither should an employee of a counselling organization be a client at the same time.

Granted that some counsellors should have counselling, should not all who want to counsel others be on the receiving end at some stage during their training? The answer is probably yes. This is not because most would-be counsellors suffer from any marked degree of psychopathology, but simply because they are human. Each of us is a unique human being, the product of what nature and nurture has made us. If we are effectively to help others at a deep personal level, we must know how we function at that level; we must become aware of our own beliefs and values, of our prejudices and 'hang-ups', and of our own story. Part of the commitment of becoming a counsellor should be to get in touch with those parts of ourselves that are least accessible, so that our own hidden agendas do not contaminate our counselling relationships with other people. Quite apart from these reasons, counsellors who have experienced counselling themselves know what it feels like to become a client; they recognize the courage it sometimes takes to ask for help; they experience some of the anxieties before the first interview; they appreciate the fear of what will be discovered; they ask the same questions about whether or not it is worth their time and their money; and (hopefully) they discover the personal enrichment that can often come from counselling. Perhaps it is for these reasons that, as often as not, it is those who through counselling have already gone through the pain of personal growth who become good counsellors themselves. While personal counselling is frequently a routine part of the preparation to become a psychotherapist, there is no tradition among the clergy that they should undergo counselling as part of their preparation for the intense pastoral work that most of them will undertake. Ordinands and clergy are unlikely to enter counselling unless they are perceived as 'having problems', and then 'having counselling' may be a condition of future employment. With all the potential advantages of increased self-awareness for pastoral ministry, it is a pity that more clergy do not make more use of this route to personal and professional growth.

The qualifications of the supervisor

Klink envisages a supervisor who is both engaged in practice and qualified to supervise. There are obvious advantages where this is possible. The supervisor both knows the setting in which counselling is carried on and has training in supervision. There are situations where this is possible, such as Klink's, which was a large psychiatric and psychotherapeutic institution with many people both engaged in practice and qualified or training to be supervisors. Such is the case in many professional settings, for example, in social work departments where those who supervise students will be qualified as social workers and possibly carry a small case-load.

Klink's vision may be a counsel of perfection in voluntary counselling agencies, as is recognized by Tyndall (1993: 61). This is particularly true in agencies which focus on pastoral counselling. For while supervisors trained in social work and psychiatry may give of themselves and their skills with a high degree of commitment, they may lack the knowledge and the experience to focus on the specifically pastoral dimensions of the task. This, however, is to anticipate a major theme of the next chapter: namely a reassessment of the distinctively pastoral nature of pastoral counselling.

In the training of clergy, a different state of affairs is likely to exist. An important feature in ministerial formation in recent years has been the development of theological field education. Training for ministry has long worked with an 'apprentice' model of training. Either during the academic course, or immediately following it, candidates for the ministry have spent time in parishes working alongside experienced ministers. Probationers and curates were given tasks to carry out; they did them and they learned from the experience. What has always been variable has been the quality of the opportunity provided for reflecting on their work. The senior ministers under whom they have served have frequently been very able pastors, ready and willing to give advice, but not at all skilled in the art of enabling reflection on practice. Recent years have seen the development of a culture in which supervision has come to be regarded as important. Many theological colleges now provide some basic training for ministers who supervise student placements. In my own denomination, the Church of Scotland, all ministers who agree to supervise probationers during their final eighteen-month-long full-time placement in a parish are expected to have attended a course on supervision. With the coming of this new understanding of supervision focusing on personal and professional growth, it can be anticipated that those currently going through the system will come to see the need for supervision not as a chore to be endured during initial training, but as an essential tool to be enjoyed throughout their ministries.

The need for commitment

Klink assumes that supervision involves a student seeking fuller qualifications for professional practice. He therefore raises issues in relation to motivation and commitment. To the extent that personal and professional growth may involve some pain, pain that results from becoming aware of shortcomings, supervision can be uncomfortable. Thus those who begin to prepare for a career either in counselling or in ministry must be sufficiently motivated to overcome this hurdle. It is important that trainees see supervision not simply as a painful experience to be endured in order to become qualified, but as the beginning of a process that will provide support and encouragement throughout their professional lives. It is also important to emphasize that supervision is essentially an *affirmative* activity. Stories are told of situations where it seemed as though a supervisor was trying to destroy the trainees. In their introduction to a symposium on *Gender Issues in Supervision*, McKenzie and Moore write:

> For anyone familiar with recent studies on the nature and dynamics of ritual process, it is evident that supervision in pastoral care and counselling has often had characteristics common to the initiation into adult masculinity, complete with ritual humiliations, etc.
>
> (McKenzie and Moore 1983: 139)

If this approach casts some doubt on the self-awareness and motivation of supervisors who function in this way, there can be no doubt about the commitment and motivation of the trainees who endure to the end. While there must inevitably be a measure of confrontation in supervision, those who come for supervision should normally go away feeling better about themselves and their developing skills. If little that is good can be said to a trainee, then some doubt must be cast on the selection procedures, not upon the trainee alone.

A contract for learning

Good supervision does not take place in a vacuum. For Klink, it is the fact that both supervisor and supervisee work within an institutional setting that makes possible the establishment of a 'Learning Agreement' which sets boundaries to the process. These boundaries not only delineate the expectations of those concerned, but also contain the anxieties generated both by the work undertaken and by supervision itself.

In any training situation, whether in preparation for pastoral ministry, or within a counselling centre, there are differing expectations, hopes, fears and anxieties. Trainees bring with them an eagerness to learn, but also uncertainties about what is expected of them and usually a realization of their own inexperience and limitations. The training centre has an awareness of the tasks waiting to be done. In the counselling centre there is usually a waiting-list of clients presenting various degrees of difficulty. In a parish setting, there are people to be visited, some of whom are experiencing deep crises in their lives. In both settings there are anxieties about matching the abilities of the trainees with the anticipated complexity of the cases on file, or the pastoral situations in the parish. There may be third parties with an interest in the outcome of a placement: for example a theological college or church committee wants assurance that students or assistant ministers are exposed to a wide variety of appropriate experiences and that they have been enabled to reflect on them.

A 'Learning Agreement' is a mechanism for bringing some cohesion into this wide diversity of expectation and anxiety. It is frequently a written document that includes agreements reached about:

- personal learning objectives of the trainee;
- tasks to be undertaken by the trainee;
- arrangements for supervision including frequency, time, place and method of presenting material for supervision.

Whether or not there is a written document, the 'contract for learning' should always embody the mutual agreement of supervisor and supervisee on how they will work together to further the professional development of the latter.

There are several ways by which learners report to supervisors on their work. A method characteristic of Clinical Pastoral Education has been the *verbatim* in which students write up as much of a conversation as they can remember. While there are obvious gaps in the recall of such conversations, much learning can take place through reflection upon what the student *thinks* went on in the conversation. This analysis is facilitated through responses to a number of carefully chosen questions, such as. What actually happened? What feelings were around in the conversation? How do you understand what was going on? What might you have done differently? How does this conversation and our reflection on it contribute to your understanding of pastoral ministry/counselling? More typical of social work is the *process report* written up as the various interviews proceed and the *case-study* written up at the conclusion of a case, though the latter can also be used effectively in training for ministry (Northcott 1990). In counselling training itself, much use has been made of *audio recordings*. This has the advantage of revealing all the verbal exchanges in a counselling session, though permission must be obtained from the client to record the interview and use it for training purposes. It is rarely possible for this method to be used in the context of the parish.

A particular problem in this context is that the keeping of detailed records, let alone the recording of pastoral conversations is alien to the way in which the clergy have traditionally functioned. While a note may be kept of the dates on which visits took place, it would not normally be part of a minister's routine to make notes for future reference about what went on during the visit. It is as though pastoral conversations were of a different nature from anything that might be termed counselling. For this reason clergy may not find it easy to adopt some aspects of professional practice should they begin to train as counsellors.

Contracts for learning are also valuable when evaluations need to be made at the end of a period of training. A statement of objectives formulated near the beginning of a placement can serve as a bench-mark against which to measure achievement. This does not mean that Learning Agreements should be carved in stone. There needs to be flexibility to modify agreements, with the consent of the parties concerned, as and when unforeseen learning needs become apparent.

So often in the past, training has not realized its full potential precisely because of a lack of clarity about objectives and methods. The existence of a contract for learning can remedy this deficiency.

Supervision and consultation

A distinction should be drawn between supervision and the related process of consultation. Normally supervision belongs to a period of professional preparation or where there is some recognized struc-ture of authority. For example, a counselling agency may insist that all its counsellors have regular supervision in proportion to their case-load. At the end of the day, the agency accepts responsibility for all who offer services in its name. It has a duty, therefore, to monitor the quality of the service offered and to further the professional development of its counsellors.

Sometimes counselling is offered in situations of great complexity and emotional stress where the helpers receive neither supervision nor support. An obvious example is to be found among the ordained ministry of the Church who routinely provide support for people in distress to a degree that few realize. In the past there was little expectation, either among themselves or others, that they would routinely seek help with their pastoral work, unless they chose to discuss difficult situations with a trusted colleague. Today there is an increased awareness of the reality of stress in parochial ministry, and of the fact that the clergy are no different from other helping professions in their need for support. Pioneering work in this field has been done by Murray Leishman and Bruce Ritson, Chaplain and Consultant Psychiatrist respectively at the Royal Edinburgh Hospital. They brought together ministers from a sector of the city on a regular basis to provide a system of support for them. Many of them worked on a long-term basis with emotionally demanding people (Leishman and Ritson 1975). But this was not supervision; it was consultation. The difference was that each minister remained responsible for his or her own work. They came to lunch-time meetings, discussed difficult situations with colleagues and the psychiatric team, and went away free to accept or reject any new insights that had come to them.

Other ministers have come to conferences on supervision in preparation for their work with probationers. As part of the training programme they have worked in *triads* or groups of three (Foskett and Lyall 1988: 154) experiencing the different roles of (a) presenting their own work; (b) helping to support a colleague; and (c) observing the process. Some have found this a valuable method of reflecting on their own ministry and have set up similar on-going arrangements with colleagues back in their parishes.

There are significant changes taking place. As more ministers benefit from good supervision in their own training and ask what it means to supervise a student or probationer entrusted to them, so will the culture change in such a way that consultation becomes a routine aspect of ministerial life. As Leishman and Ritson conclude:

Far from being a luxury this activity enables clergy to meet the patients'/parishioners' needs more exactly than before i.e. in the provision of an appropriate support system. That is, to paraphrase St Paul, that we may be able to support those who are in any trouble by the support wherewith we ourselves are supported. There is no elite in this process.

(Leishman and Ritson 1975: 24)

Gender issues in supervision

Until comparatively recently, little attention has been given to how relationships between women and men influence the processes of counselling and supervision. There is evidence that this issue is now being taken more seriously. In a article on 'Gender and Counselling', Jocelyn Chaplin (1993) explores how gender shapes counselling both in terms of the processes involved in the different possible permutations of the male/female relationship and in terms of content. Process issues are related to power struggles between women and men. Content issues relate to gender roles, bodily awareness and sexuality in counselling. In a companion to this volume, Janet Perry (1993) writes about counselling services for women. What they describe about the counselling relationship has obvious implications for the process.

In 1983, the *Journal of Supervision and Training in Ministry* published a symposium on gender issues in supervision. One article on 'The Emergence of Feminine Consciousness in Supervision', written by two women (a supervisor and a supervisee), draws attention to what they believe to be a radically different approach, one that is rooted in the women's movement. They attempted to establish a style of supervision that is 'relational, collaborative, and collegial', lacking neither intellectual rigour nor good organization. Both point to deficiencies in the traditional male model in which:

> 'Good supervision' requires sharp and clear boundary distinctions between teacher and student . . .' 'Good supervision' is supposed to 'hurt good' meaning that the supervisor keeps the student at an optimum level of anxiety in order to soften rigid defence structures and keep the emotional investment of the student at its peak.

(Jewett and Haight 1983: 172)

In contrast, they demonstrate how under the collegial model, students reported finding it easier to establish a strong professional identity. Further, their less confrontational approach resulted in a voluntary lowering of defences induced by the high level of respect and trust expressed by the supervisor. In attempting to understand at a cognitive level why the collegial approach was more effective, Emily Haight finds a clue in the experience of being pregnant and giving birth. At first she rebelled at the loss of control she felt over the creative activity of her body, but in time this gave way to a different feeling:

> The deeply rooted image of nurturing another by co-operating with rather than controlling its unique and innate developmental process became a metaphor for the supervisory relationship.
>
> (Jewett and Haight 1983: 172)

This understanding of supervision grows out of women's experience. Yet if it is a distinctively feminine perspective, its application need not be confined to counselling and supervisory relationships involving women. It is a good example of an approach generated by the feminine consciousness which has relevance for all human relationships. There are indications that feminine perspectives will be able to bring new insights to our understanding of pastoral relationships. More and more women are being ordained to pastoral office in the churches; the majority of those who train as counsellors in this context are women. These facts alone will surely help to counter the difficulties found in most religious contexts of breaking away from male, hierarchical models of ministry.

In this chapter I have examined a number of areas where there are clear parallels between counselling in the pastoral and spiritual context, and counselling in other contexts. I have noted that even where there is a commonality of interest, the context influences the way in which problems present themselves. While most of the issues discussed have been raised most acutely in the field of pastoral counselling, there have inevitably been important implications for the closely related discipline of pastoral care. Issues of confidentiality and of boundaries, sexual and otherwise, have always been of implicit significance in ministries of pastoral care. The fact that they have been raised much more explicitly in pastoral counselling may also lead to a more thoughtful and deliberate delivery of pastoral care.

I now turn to a consideration of issues specific to the pastoral and spiritual context. Not surprisingly, the main issue is religion and therein lies both the problem and the potential.

· FOUR ·

Specific issues in counselling in the pastoral and spiritual context

A recurring theme in previous chapters has been the way in which religious beliefs, spiritual experience and personal values impinge on helping relationships. More detailed consideration of this matter is important for a number of reasons. First, in the pastoral and spiritual context, an understanding of what it means to be human cannot be contained solely within psychological models. A study of the varieties of religious experience, both within the Christian and other religious traditions, reveals that integral to each is a distinctive understanding of personhood, of what it means to be a person who is fully human. Second, among those counselling within this context there are a variety of opinions as to whether there are therapeutic resources that are quite specific to the context. At one extreme there are the Christian counsellors who believe that their main resources are to be found in scripture and prayer; there are also holistic therapies that value meditation and centring on forces outside the self; there are pastoral counselling centres functioning with a Christian ethos that is more implicit than explicit; and there are counsellors and therapists in other settings to whom spiritual ideas are important, but who do not reveal these explicitly in their work with clients. Indeed, it can be argued that there is *no* context in which the beliefs and values of counsellors and their clients do not impinge in some way on their relationship. To look at this issue, therefore, in a context where it is clearly relevant, may well shed some light on the same issue as it appears in other contexts.

In this context, therefore, there are critical issues relating to religion and spirituality. For some these present a problem and for others they are considered to be of potential therapeutic value.

Religion as a problem

A recent history of the Westminster Pastoral Foundation (Black 1991) illustrates the 'problem' of religion for pastoral counselling. I described in Chapter One how Bill Kyle's original vision for the WPF was that it should become a church-based pastoral counselling centre. In the early training courses, the overtly religious dimension was very strong, a pattern which was to continue for the first six or seven years. However, with increasing psychotherapeutic sophistication, the Foundation's understanding of the word 'pastoral' became problematic. Black devotes a whole chapter of his book to the 'Pastoral/Clinical Debate'. He begins by noting that:

> as the 1970s wore on, many religious professionals found in WPF, a way of moving towards a largely or entirely secular career, and secular professionals found a new field in which to teach and develop their expertise.
>
> (Black 1991: 61)

Black describes the intensity that surrounded WPF's debate about the word 'pastoral' and how it occupied much of the best energies of the staff, when they stood back from their immediate work and tried to consider what they were 'really about'. A critical incident seems to have been the different responses in a supervision group to one trainee, a nun, who reported that she had prayed with a client. Some saw this as an expression of role confusion on the part of the trainee counsellor. The supervisor himself saw the event rather differently. In his view two languages, one religious and the other psychodynamic, were being used to describe the same inner reality. Ways had to be found for relating them to one another. He refused to go along with the tacit blurring or relegation of religious beliefs which so often accompanied the move towards psycho-dynamic interpretations, but his view was not the dominant one.

Within WPF, other responses to the pastoral/clinical debate were less clear-cut. Some thought that 'pastoral' care was care that approaches another with awe as well as love and well-informed understanding. Others again saw the contribution of religion to their work as in some way 'inspirational'. Most recently there has been a move towards the affirmation of the clinical at the expense of the pastoral:

> To move on from the Bill Kyle era . . . a new argument has prevailed: that, indeed, what is done and taught in WPF is not pastoral counselling. WPF, which now trains few clergy, is teaching and practising a secular activity to which the word pastoral

has no application. Consonant with this the word has been dropped from our official description of the work we do, which is now called psychotherapy or psychodynamic counselling, and is maintained in our organisational title only to maintain continuity with our roots.

(Black 1991: 64)

This case-study demonstrates the difficulty of maintaining an overtly pastoral dimension while pursuing high standards of excellence in psychotherapy. This does not mean that many of the therapists do not have their own deeply held religious beliefs. Many of them probably do and the perspective that flows from these beliefs infuses their whole approach to others. In such situations the pastoral counsellor is no different from the Christian surgeon whose beliefs are never made explicit in his relationship with patients, even though these beliefs may greatly influence both his attitude towards his patients and his stance on ethical issues.

The contribution of WPF to counselling in Britain has been an important one. Their training is a model for many others and the establishment of the network of affiliated and associated centres has been an important resource for the development of counselling in churches and communities throughout the country. Nevertheless, in an emphasis on the clinical at the expense of the pastoral, something of value may be lost. A legitimate concern to respect the autonomy of the counsellee may lead to an undervaluing of some aspects of human experience which, when properly acknowledged and responded to, can be significant for the counselling process.

Religion as therapeutic potential

I wish to argue that a distinctive function of counselling in the pastoral and spiritual context must be to take religious experience seriously. If counsellors in this context cannot acknowledge the pervasive nature of this aspect of what it means to be human, and be comfortable in their response to it, then there can be little expectation that counsellors in any other context will. I suggest that there are three factors that indicate that counsellors should not undervalue religious experience. These relate to (a) the universality of human religious experience; (b) the diagnostic value of religious ideas; and (c) the therapeutic potential of religious faith.

(a)   Recent research points to the *universality of human religious experience*. In *Exploring Inner Space*, Hay (1987) describes how nearly 3000 people were asked whether they had ever had 'a feeling that somehow you were ever in the presence of God' (p. 120). Over two-thirds of the sample responded positively. Not only that, but both British and American studies demonstrate that about a quarter of those who never go to church respond positively to the question 'Have you ever been aware of or influenced by a presence or power?' (p. 132). Hay's research has indicated that the phenomenon of religious *experience* is far more widespread, in and out of church, among all sections of the population than was previously acknowledged.

Sometimes, counsellors working in secular agencies find that religious issues can be of great importance to their clients. In bereavement counselling, it may not be possible to avoid the exploration of attitudes to death and the afterlife, or of guilt and judgement, simply because these are matters that are raised by the client.

Again, there are occasions when someone may seek a pastoral counsellor precisely out of a desire to explore faith issues in a manner not possible in a secular context. A college chaplain became involved in a pastoral relationship with a postgraduate theological student who was concurrently in psychotherapy, an arrangement that was cleared with and welcomed by the young man's therapist. When the psychotherapy came to an end, the analyst wrote up the case for a professional meeting, stating that the student ' "seduced" the chaplain into "talking theology" sessions'. What is interesting in the therapist's case-presentation is the assumption that for the student and the chaplain to have engaged in 'talking theology' must necessarily be classified as seduction. It could have been. In the context of a psychoanalytic relationship it arguably might have been. But in the context of the pastoral relationship there was no reason why it should be, and in this particular case it probably was not. It *would* have been easy for the chaplain to be seduced into a sterile discussion of academic theology. The reality was that the student's dissertation was 'stuck' and that his 'stuckness' had a great deal to do with who and where he was as a person. But the chaplain was neither the student's therapist nor his academic supervisor. He saw his role as primarily being a minister to the student, and secondly of allowing him to set the agenda for an exploration of the interface between the academic and personal issues that would both be fed back into his therapy and enable him to get on with his writing. In fact (and we must guard against confusing coincidence with causality) the student began to make rapid progress with his research and completed his doctorate.

It must also be recognized that when counsellees come for help to a setting which in any way is designated 'pastoral', they bring to the counselling something of their previous religious experience.

When people come to what is known to be a church-related centre, or enter a pastoral relationship with a minister or priest, past experiences, good or bad, with clergy, with the Church and with God may influence the counselling relationship. For example, the initial responses of patients when I introduced myself as 'the hospital chaplain' were often fascinating. 'I'm not a religious person' or 'I don't got to church but . . .' were common responses. One old lady reached for her purse! Other patients spoke openly about how prayer had helped them in previous crises or about how much the prayers of others had meant to them. These past religious experiences may need to be brought into the open and explored, pastor and patient together, if their relationship is to be optimally helpful.

There is a natural and proper reticence among counsellors to avoid imposing their own beliefs upon clients. It is a pity, however, if this admirable quality prevents religious experience being part of the totality of human experience which is available for exploration.

(b)   The second reason why counsellors should not undervalue religious experience is to be found in the evidence that religious ideas can be an *aid to diagnosis*. Draper *et al.* (1965) undertook research that involved taking a full religious history from a group of patients. Among the questions asked were: What is your earliest memory of religious experience or belief? What is your favourite Bible story? Why? What does prayer mean to you? If you pray, what do you pray about? What do you consider the greatest sin one could commit? On the basis of the answers to these and similar questions *alone*, a team of psychiatrists was asked to make a diagnosis of the patient's illness. Frequently (in ninety-two per cent of cases), this coincided with the diagnosis made on more conventional grounds. This clearly indicates that the religious history of an individual is not something separate from the story of a person's whole life. Draper's research has been used as the basis for instruments attempting some kind of spiritual assessment of patients or clients (Fitchett 1993: 9). This has assumed increasing importance within the North American Health Care system where every service offered, even pastoral care, has to be justified in financial terms. Even where such restraints do not exist, pastoral counsellors who work in interdisciplinary teams (for example, chaplains in psychiatric hospitals) need to be skilled in exploring this aspect of human experience. The spiritual journey of the client is nearly always a reflection of important themes in that person's life. It is surely a paradox that, in an age when the most intimate details of a client's family and sexual history are openly discussed, there should be a reticence about exploring details of the faith journey.

(c)   In this context particularly we must explore *the therapeutic potential of religious resources*. At this point we enter more controversial territory. It is perhaps significant that in his seminal work on pastoral counselling, Seward Hiltner (1949) did not deal with the issue of religious resources such as prayer, the use of scripture and sacraments until the penultimate chapter. On the one hand his primary concern was to set down the theory and practice of good counselling, drawing on what he considers the best of the secular therapies. On the other he did not want to exclude the use of resources rooted in the Christian pastoral tradition. This ambivalence is understandable and will always exist within the pastoral counsellor who respects the autonomy of the client. It may be resolved in different ways, and not always to the advantage of the counsellee. If, on the one hand, 'Christian counsellors' tend to rush in too quickly with scriptural answers, on the other, counsellors working in a secular arena may underestimate the significance of a religious faith in the lives of their clients.

Behind these issues there are deeper ones relating both to our understanding of human nature and of what we believe to be the nature of pastoral counselling. I propose to use one theological understanding of human anxiety as a springboard for exploring some important issues in pastoral counselling. This is followed by an account of some approaches to pastoral counselling in terms of their dominant metaphors or controlling ideas.

HUMAN ANXIETY IN PASTORAL PERSPECTIVE

The modern theologian who has entered into the most constructive dialogue with secular psychotherapy is undoubtedly Paul Tillich. A major contribution to that dialogue was his analysis of the nature of human anxiety in *The Courage to Be* (1952):

> I suggest that we distinguish three types of anxiety according to the three directions in which non-being threatens being. Non-being threatens man's ontic self-affirmation (*i.e. his very being*), relatively in terms of fate, absolutely in terms of death. It threatens man's spiritual self-affirmation, relatively in terms of emptiness, absolutely in terms of meaninglessness. It threatens man's moral self-affirmation, relatively in terms of guilt, absolutely in terms of condemnation. The awareness of this three-fold threat is anxiety appearing in three forms, that of fate and death (briefly the anxiety of death), that of emptiness

and loss of meaning (briefly, the anxiety of meaninglessness), that of guilt and condemnation (briefly, the anxiety of condemnation). In all three forms anxiety is existential in the sense that it belongs to existence as such and not to a normal state of mind as in neurotic (and psychotic) anxiety.

(Tillich 1952: 49)

While death, meaninglessness and the threat of condemnation do not limit the issues that form the agenda for counselling in the pastoral and spiritual context, they are often present. Again I illustrate from my own work as a hospital chaplain.

I can think of a young man crippled by a road-traffic accident which was not his fault, his life irrevocably changed and limited, who inevitably found his fate hard to accept. Many patients admitted to an oncology ward saw themselves, rightly or wrongly, as walking through the valley of the shadow of death. Parents who had lost a child invariably found it hard to make sense of what had happened to them. Degenerative neurological disease can provoke a profound sense of meaninglessness. I once introduced myself to a patient in a neurological ward who could only communicate through typing with one finger. He laboriously spelt out the letters w-h-y-d-o-e-s-g-o-d-a-l-l-o-w- and then burst into tears.

Sometimes, patients express the feeling that they are being condemned for something they have done in the past. One woman in her seventies, in hospital being treated for cancer of the cervix, approached the chaplain after a service. She had read in a magazine that there was a relationship between this kind of cancer and sexual promiscuity, Once, forty years before, when her husband had been away during the war, she had been unfaithful to him. She felt that God was now punishing her. While she may have been suffering from depression in relation to her illness, it is also true that people find it easier to believe in what they perceive as God's justice than His love. 'We'll pay for it' is a common expression in my own Scottish culture but it is an idea that is widespread. In T. S. Eliot's play, *The Cocktail Party*, Celia Copplestone says in her confession to the psychiatrist:

It's not the feeling of anything I have ever *done*
Which I might get away from, or of anything in me
I could get rid of – but of emptiness, of failure
Toward someone, or something, outside of myself;
And I feel I must . . . *atone* – is that the word?

(Eliot 1950)

It might be argued that it is more than forty years since Tillich in his theology and Eliot in his drama set out their analysis of the human condition. Much in the world has changed since then. To what extent are their insights still valid for pastoral counselling?

The acceptance of death

It can be argued that public attitudes to death have changed. As recently as 1970, a paper was published in the *British Medical Journal* indicating that while eighty per cent of terminally ill patients knew they were dying and would like to talk about it, eighty per cent of doctors denied this and believed that patients should not be told (Cramond 1970: 389). Since then at least two factors have helped to change professional, if not cultural, attitudes to death. First, the modern hospice movement pioneered by Cecily Saunders has brought the care of the dying to the forefront of public consciousness. Quite apart from the contribution of the hospices themselves, the dissemination of their philosophy has strengthened the hands of those working in other institutions who have long fought for resources to provide high-quality care where cure was not possible. Second, the ideas of the Swiss-American doctor Elisabeth Kubler-Ross, embodied in her book *On Death and Dying* (1969), have led to a new understanding of the emotional reactions of those facing their own death, and indeed of people suffering any major loss. There can be few in any of the caring professions who are not familiar with her 'five stages', commonly observed in those who are aware that their life is coming to an end: denial, anger, bargaining, depression and acceptance. This intellectual framework for trying to understand the feelings of those who face the ultimate loss has its own value, although it is recognized that individuals cannot always be fitted neatly into these stages. The mystery of death and dying cannot be contained within a diagram in a book. Further, those who counsel the dying almost certainly have to come to terms with their feelings about the important losses in their own lives and their own mortality (in so far as anyone can). Nowhere in the process of supervision is it more important to help counsellors move beyond intellectual understanding to self-awareness. These are traditional religious concerns, and remain so, even in a largely secular (white) Western society.

Meaning and postmodernism

From deep within her sense of emptiness Celia Copplestone also spoke of 'failure ... Toward someone, or something outside of myself'. Despite her own feelings of desolation, she implied that it was possible to find a sense of meaning and purpose for her life. A dominant voice in contemporary philosophy is that no such sense of meaning and purpose is possible. While neither clients nor parishioners are likely to have heard of postmodernism, the values of that philosophy permeate our culture. If modernism was underwritten by the belief that it *was* possible to find meaning, and that meaning could be found in science and rationality, the postmodern ideology is that there are no ideologies. There are no 'metanarratives', no big stories, no grand plans or theories, even in theory, into which 'everything fits'. The only ultimate reality is death.

The New Testament scholar, James Breech, describes the demoralizing pressures on 'the project of making a whole out of one's life' (Kelber 1983: 73):

> On the most obvious level, the idea is that people are 'demoral-ized' in the sense that their moralities are relativized . . . But for those who share the postmodern conviction that death is God, demoralization in the sense of despair would appear to be the expected outcome.
>
> (Breech 1989: 19)

Drawing on the writings of Christopher Lasch (1984), Breech paints a portrait of the self that has implications for pastoral counselling:

> Lasch shows how the contemporary self, uncertain of its own outlines, is lost in a world of flickering images, unable to tell the difference between fantasy and reality. Selfhood is equated with the ability to play a variety of roles and to assume an endless variety of chosen identities. Gone according to Lasch, is any notion of stability in identity, or any sense of one's life 'as a life history or narrative'. . . . Psychic survivors travel light; there is no room for a personal life or a personal history.
>
> (Breech 1989: 20)

Postmodernism presents a challenge to pastoral counselling in two ways. There is a challenge to the extent that every client or parishioner has a story to tell. Sometimes that story is told through the taking of a formal case-history from a client; at other times a parishioner begins by saying 'Well, minister, to let you understand, it was like this . . .' and launches into his or her story. Although their stories may not make much sense to them at that moment, and the pervasive, cultural pressures of postmodernism militate against even believing that it is possible to find meaning in them, people tell their stories in the attempt to make sense of their

experience. In this respect they are much more in tune with another trend in contemporary philosophy and theology, a movement
indeed which believes that human experience can only be understood in terms of narrative. In his seminal paper on 'The Narrative
Quality of Experience', Stephen Crites (1971) argues that one of the
conditions for being human is the capacity for being aware of having a personal history. Our lives find meaning, says Crites, in the
interaction between the *mundane stories* of our lives, the 'little stories'
which give expression to our own personal experience and the
sacred stories of our culture, the 'big stories' we all share.

It is here that we meet the second challenge of postmodernism,
the challenge to *pastoral* counselling. As we saw when we examined
the different religious traditions, there is at the heart of each a 'big
story' or group of stories which sets apart that faith from all others.
This is certainly true of the Christian faith. Rooted in the history of
the Jews, its sacred scriptures tell stories of a remarkable man who
himself communicated through telling stories. If these stories are
formative of the Christian tradition, then we certainly need to explore
the extent to which they are important for any counselling that takes
place within a community so constituted. The same is true of the
Jewish tradition. In a paper on 'Symbols and Healing: A Personal
Perspective on Analysis', David Freeman, a Rabbi and Jungian analyst
writes:

> The stories, liturgy and rituals of Judaism are the heritage of
> every Jew and they carry inside them the collective experience
> of his and her people, and of the whole Jewish people! The
> ritual of 'Shiva' (of mourning the dead) and the saying of
> 'Kaddish' (the prayer recited for the dead) are often a container
> which holds, transforms and heals the family grief. At the *Seder*
> table each Jew is commanded to imagine it as if they had
> personally gone out of Egypt.
>
> (Freeman 1988: 207)

Islam, Hinduism and Buddhism also have their sacred stories which
are formative of the collective experience and which have shaped
the cultural values of members of these communities. They provide
a framework within which the stories of individual lives find meaning, and therefore constitute at least part of the context for counselling within these religious traditions.

Sin and guilt

Celia Copplestone spoke not only of emptiness but of failure and
the need to atone. In this allusion to atonement, T. S. Eliot set this

woman's conversation with the psychiatrist in the context of traditional Christian concepts of sin and guilt. It has been said, sometimes with a degree of truth, that while the Christian religion has shackled men and women with its emphasis on sin and guilt, psychoanalysis has been the great liberator. We do not need to look far to find evidence demonstrating both the guilt-inducing properties of religion and the enhanced personal freedom which has resulted from psychotherapy.

Yet different voices have been heard. Some have alleged that, far from emphasizing guilt, the contemporary Church has succumbed to the ethos of contemporary, psychologized culture and neglected its own traditional message of sin and salvation. I am not referring here to pronouncements coming from conservative branches of the Church, for that is what we would expect to hear from these sources anyway, but to voices speaking from within psychology and psychotherapy. When O. Hobart Mowrer, then Professor of Psychology at the University of Illinois, wrote *The Crisis in Psychiatry and Religion* (1961), for him, that crisis was the denial by men and women of responsibility for their own actions and that real guilt was being reduced to neurotic guilt. He maintained there was great therapeutic potential in an alliance between religion and psychiatry which emphasized the need for confession and restitution. Confession led to the acceptance of personal responsibility and restitution to the relief of a guilty conscience. These ideas were fundamental to Mowrer's Integrity Therapy which functioned through peer self-help psychotherapy groups (Drakeford 1990: 585). Neither is the concept of reparation alien to psychoanalytic thinking. Rycroft (1972) defines reparation as a defence mechanism for reducing guilt by action designed to make good the harm imagined to have been done to others; he notes that in Kleinian thinking there is a tendency to regard all creative activity as reparative.

A similar view was expressed by Karl Menninger, a co-founder and former Director of the Menninger Clinic in Topeka, Kansas. Some years ago, Menninger, then in his eighties, addressed an interdisciplinary group of doctors, nurses, social workers and chaplains at the psychiatric hospital in Edinburgh. His opening gambit was 'Where are the chaplains?' He then proceeded to ask the chaplains present, including the author, to give an account of themselves and their role within the National Health Service. As administrator, author and therapist he made an immense contribution to the advancement of psychoanalysis in the United States. He was also a Presbyterian elder who gave great support to the development of new modes of pastoral counselling which were divorced from the moralistic attitudes underpinning much of the pastoral care of the past. But in his book *Whatever Became of Sin?* (Menninger 1973), something of his Calvinist background became evident. While affirming the importance of psychodynamic insights for both psychotherapy and pastoral counselling, he also argued that there were such things as moral concern and personal responsibility, and that the acknowledgement of these truths by psychologists and physicians was of therapeutic importance:

> Is it not possible that some of their patients, deeply involved in self-destructive or socially destructive activities are seeking help for minor symptoms which disguise major sins? Is it possible that some thus attempt to atone with money and suffering for all the sins they are – or are not – confessing? We would condemn clergymen for offering only pastoral counsel as therapy to a man suffering from brain syphilis or 'schizophrenia'. Would we withhold all censure from a psychiatrist who is giving psychotherapy for 'neurotic' symptoms of sleeplessness or sexual inhibition to a man involved in rascality or wickedness to a notable degree?
>
> (Menninger 1973: 49)

Menninger believed that his thesis was essentially hopeful:

> Therefore I say that the consequence of my proposal would not be more depression but less. If the concept of personal responsibility and answerability for ourselves and for others were to return to common acceptance, hope would return to the world with it!
>
> (Menninger 1973: 188)

Such distinctive contributions by people of the stature of Mowrer and Menninger certainly give a fresh twist to the dialogue between psychiatry and religion. While their views do not command universal assent they have provoked a degree of controversy within the psychotherapeutic community. A careful analysis of the phenomenon of guilt was needed from someone who commanded both theological and psychological credibility. It came from E. V. Stein, Professsor of Pastoral Psychology at San Francisco Theological Seminary, and included a response to Mowrer.

In *Guilt: Theory and Therapy* (1968) Stein maintains that Mowrer had done a service to psychology and psychotherapy in forcing consideration of the importance of values and of real guilt. He also feels that Mowrer has overstated his case. He argues that Mowrer caricatured Freud in stating that the latter did not take guilt seriously.

Further, Mowrer took a moralistic view of neurosis and did not
realize the danger of putting extra burdens upon people already
feeling worthless and full of self-hate. Such a legalistic understanding
of the relationship between suffering, punishment and forgiveness
runs contrary both to a theological understanding of grace and to
psychotherapeutic integrity. Finally, Mowrer did not differentiate
sufficiently between real guilt and neurotic guilt. Stein demonstrates
that these were two quite different entities. Neurotic guilt is to be
understood as inappropriate feelings of guilt about aspects of the
personality that are integral to being human in a healthy way (for
example, sexuality, self-assertion and self-love); real guilt is appropriate remorse over past actions. He also distinguishes each of these
manifestations of guilt from the complete absence of any appropriate sense of guilt which can occur in the sociopathic personality.

Stein maintains that different kinds of guilt feelings demand different pastoral responses:

> To treat *neurotic* guilt on a confessional, reality basis is to reject
> the counselee and to identify with his tormentors, internal and
> historical . . . To treat *real* guilt on the other hand as *neurotic*
> and something 'that cannot be helped' is, as Mowrer makes
> clear, to cauterize moral sensitivity and to undermine human
> community and the hard-won values of the human race in the
> name of science.
>
> (Stein 1968: 147)

Stein has continued to write of the pastoral task in counselling
clients who feel burdened by guilt.

> The aim of the pastoral counseling of guilt is to help the guilty
> person discern the real and/or neurotic quality of the guilt, deal
> therapeutically with the latter, and, where existential guilt is
> present, help the person appropriate, assimilate and share God's
> love, forgiveness and acceptance, moving toward personal and
> communal wholeness.
>
> (Stein 1990: 491)

Thus we can identify two possible pastoral responses to feelings
of guilt in counsellees. Pastoral counsellors might appropriately use
either or both but there is a clear responsibility upon the counsellor
to discern what kind of guilt is being expressed. In the case of
existential guilt and remorse, there is also the need to take account
of the belief system of the counsellee regarding the practice of confession. Helping a counsellee 'appropriate, assimilate and share God's
love, forgiveness and acceptance' often involves a finely balanced

decision, to be shared with the counsellee, about whether this can be done in the context of the counselling relationship or needs to be referred to a priest for confession and absolution in a manner familiar and meaningful for the counsellee.

From guilt to shame

In recent years there has been a significant movement in the debate about guilt, with a shift in emphasis to another closely related emotion, namely, shame.

Donald Capps calls the first chapter of his book *The Depleted Self: Sin in a Narcissistic Age* (1993), 'Whatever Became of Sin?', recalling the above-mentioned book by Menninger. An initial enthusiasm for Menninger's book did not last, and Capps attributes this to the fact that Menninger 'did not address the deep and pervasive psychocultural reasons why sin seems to have so little meaning for us today' (Capps 1993: 5). In *The Culture of Narcissism* (1979), Christopher Lasch argues that the dominant personality of our time is narcissistic and that this new self is haunted not by guilt but by an anxiety which has nothing to do with guilt.

> Guilt has not simply been repressed. The axis around which the narcissistic self turns is not guilt but shame.
>
> (Capps 1993: 7)

Later, Capps spells out the difference between guilt and shame:

> shame is a response to our failure to live up to an ideal we have held for ourselves and that shame is therefore an experience of a self-deficiency . . . We are disappointed in ourselves. We have once again let ourselves down, and are puzzled and angry with ourselves: 'Why do I do this to myself?' This reaction is quite different from guilt, for, with guilt, the ideals that we have failed to live up to we continue to associate with the expectations of others.
>
> (Capps 1993: 72)

It should be noted in passing that this absence of guilt in the narcissistic personality is not the same as that exhibited by sociopathic personalities, which the psychiatric literature classifies as a 'character disorder'. If the narcissistic personality has substituted shame for guilt, in the psychopathic personality both guilt *and* shame are absent.

If shame has indeed replaced guilt as a source of anxiety, this has implications for pastoral counselling. It would be easy to jump on

a bandwagon and to imagine that counsellors will no longer encounter clients who experience the kind of guilt feelings identified
by Tillich and Stein. This is manifestly not so. However, Capps
argues that in a period when pastoral theology was preoccupied
with guilt, the experience of shame was repressed and absorbed
into guilt. When shame is recognized as being a component of
anxiety, certainly talk of confession and forgiveness is of little value.
When, however, shame is experienced as a gap between what we
are and what we would like to be, between an actual self and an
ideal self, then a starting-point for any counselling must involve an
understanding of this bipolarity.

Contemporary understanding of the narcissistic personality owes
much to the self-psychology of Heinz Kohut, for whom the self was
essentially bipolar with ambitions and drives in tension with values
and ideals. This does not differ essentially from the theological
anthropology expressed by St Paul when he wrote 'I do not do
what I want, but I do the very thing I hate' (Romans, 7: 15, RSV).
On Kohut's contribution to pastoral care, Homer Ashby writes:

> Through Kohut's thinking, we have an improved understanding
> of the intrapsychic process by which the self's values and ideals
> emerge. According to self-psychology, these values and ideals
> emerge out of the context of the relationship between the child
> and its parent(s) . . . The pastoral care field is also interested in
> the contexts which shape and consolidate values, ideals and
> value meanings. Are these two value or ideal contexts the same
> or different? If so, how so? My own belief is that they are
> directly related and share a common ontology. Those values
> and ideals which shape the parent–child interaction flow from
> the values, ideals and moral context which have been formed
> and influenced by the larger society. No person or culture is
> immune from such moral, value or ideal influence. It is *within*
> the framework of this larger moral context that the self develops
> its ideals and values in intimate relationship with others.
>
> (Ashby 1982: 154)

This recognition of the importance of 'the values, ideals and moral
context which have been formed and influenced by the larger society' is entirely congruent with Stephen Crites' emphasis on the
place of sacred stories in the formation of human consciousness.
Thus if shame is an issue to be addressed in the context of counselling, an exploration of values is not irrelevant. Becoming aware
of the relationship between our own values and ideals and those of

the larger society may lead to an exploration of our own mundane story in relation to the sacred stories of the culture. That these sacred stories speak of One whose unconditional acceptance of us *as we are* may not be without therapeutic significance. If, however, this is a major theme of the sacred story that shapes the values and ideals of counselling in the pastoral and spiritual context, what does this mean in practice?

Behind every method of counselling in the pastoral and spiritual context there is an understanding of what it means to be human. Having become aware of the limitations of older theological models, pastoral counsellors are perhaps too uncritical in their acceptance of newer psychological models. More recently, however, pastoral counselling has found a renewed confidence in its own metaphors. Psychological insights have their place, but they are not given priority. They are incorporated in such a way that the bringing together of different perspectives gives a fuller and deeper understanding of people. What are the implications for the practice of pastoral counselling?

THE METAPHORS OF PASTORAL COUNSELLING

Contemporary pastoral care and counselling is dependent neither on a single psychological theory nor on one theological system. Nor does it find expression in one practical approach. I now wish to explore some of the ways in which pastoral counsellors understand what they are doing in the face-to-face encounter with a parishioner or client. Some of these have been alluded to in previous chapters. Four such approaches can be described in terms of a dominant metaphor which characterizes each of them. These are:

(a) pastoral counselling as proclamation;
(b) pastoral counselling as therapy;
(c) pastoral counselling as story-telling;
(d) pastoral counselling as companionship.

Pastoral counselling as proclamation

For some, to speak of any kind of counselling in terms of proclamation is a contradiction in terms. Indeed, so to speak is to confirm the worst fears of those who think that religion and counselling should be kept as far apart as possible. Nevertheless, this approach goes back a long way and I have shown in Chapter Two how it finds recent expression in the work of the Swiss pastor Eduard Thurneysen. For him pastoral care is the preaching of the Gospel to the individual and the sole content of the proclamation is the forgiveness of sin. Underlying the metaphor of preaching is the assumption that 'man' is a sinner under judgement who needs to hear the word of grace. The insights of psychology and psychotherapy are not to be neglected but these are 'auxiliary sciences', making no essential contribution to a 'real' understanding of man. This merely clears the way for the presentation of the good news. This model had a dominating influence in Protestant Europe, and when Thurneysen's *A Theology of Pastoral Care* (1962) was translated into English it gave credence to the established practice of many pastors. Under the influence of new psychological insights, its shortcomings were exposed. Burck (1978) has described a two-stage transformation in this approach.

The first stage was to challenge the assumption that the *only* content of the message was that of forgiveness:

> Thurneysen's emphasis on forgiveness erred theologically in that it ignored the breadth of human meaning and of human responsiveness to life in the dimensions of creation and redemption, e.g. joy, peace, love, hope, kindness and a responsible communication of the gospel.
>
> (Burck 1978: 221)

It makes little sense, for instance, to speak of sin and forgiveness to someone struggling to come to terms with the givenness of his or her sexuality. If there is a 'word' to be spoken it should probably be about the goodness of God in creation. But if the first stage in the transformation of this model is a broadening of the content of the proclamation, a second stage leads to the emergence of a totally new paradigm for pastoral care. Joachim Scharfenberg, a German Professor of Practical Theology and a qualified psychoanalyst, understands pastoral care as **dialogue** (1987). His theological method is to look for the specifically pastoral within the structure of the conversation. The aim of pastoral conversation is to enable the client to find personal freedom, and in this respect pastoral conversation draws on the insights of psychoanalysis. The theological nature of the pastoral conversation is still important, but now 'the word' is not imposed upon the conversation but allowed to emerge from it. This 'therapeutic model' of pastoral care 'creates space' in which the counsellee arrives at his/her own theological understandings:

The pastor is there to make room for the partner's concerns; he is there to start with the human, not to make room for the message from God.

(Burck 1978: 226)

One of my central arguments is that pastoral counsellors must be willing and able to respond in an appropriate manner to human religious experience and belief. This new paradigm for pastoral counselling would seem to do justice both to the integrity of that experience and to the principles of good counselling. It acknowledges the reality of spiritual experience, and the need of counsellees to make sense of it, either in terms of their present beliefs or by modifying them. But no attempt is made to say *how* that experience is to be interpreted. Rather, the counselling relationship provides the freedom in which clients can make their own interpretations. A man was referred for bereavement counselling by his GP six months after his father had been killed in a road traffic accident. While accepting the death intellectually, the client believed that if it could be proved that the accident had been caused by the other driver, his father would return. During counselling, he recounted a recent dream. Both he and his father were at a funeral and while he could not sing the hymns his father did so with enthusiasm. On being asked by the counsellor what sense he made of the dream, his response was that while he was still 'stuck', his father was 'all right'. From that point the fantasy about the return of his father became less intense.

Sometimes the interpretation may be pathological, as in the case, recounted earlier, of the woman who believed that her cancer was God's punishment for her single lapse of marital infidelity many years before. As I indicated, this interpretation may be the expression of a depressive illness. Whether or not this is so, it is probable that little will be gained by easy talk of sin and forgiveness. However, having attempted to model understanding and acceptance in the counselling relationship, the counsellor should not exclude the possibility that, at the end of the day, for a client with deep religious convictions it is precisely the experience of confession and absolution which helps them to move on. What is important is that this should not be imposed on the client by the counsellor, either directly or subtly, but should emerge from the pastoral conversation itself as a preferred way forward.

Thus, what at first sight appears a very directive model of pastoral counselling can be transformed into one with therapeutic relevance. It is also possible, however, for some essentially non-directive, secular approaches to be incorporated within a pastoral theological perspective.

Pastoral counselling as therapy

In speaking of a therapeutic model of pastoral counselling, I am referring to those developments, originating mainly in North America, which draw heavily upon the ethos and methods of the proliferating secular psychotherapies. I described in Chapter One the enormous impetus given to pastoral counselling through the adoption of such ideas and practices. I also noted how pastoral counselling tends to drift away from its moorings within the traditional ministries of the Church. Paul Tillich is aware of this danger. In a paper on 'The Theology of Pastoral Care' (1959), he builds on his analysis of human anxiety which he articulated in *The Courage to Be*. He sees the answer to human finitude, guilt and doubt in 'acceptance'. Acceptance is of central importance in all the major psychotherapies, but Tillich points beyond the acceptance of the counselling relationship to a deeper kind of acceptance. In a famous sermon he said:

> Sometimes . . . a wave of light breaks into our darkness, and it is as though a voice were saying: 'You are accepted. *You are accepted*, accepted by that which is greater than you, and the name of which you do not know. Do not ask for the name now; perhaps you will find it later. Do not try to do anything now; perhaps later you will do much. Do not seek for anything; do not perform anything; do not intend anything. *Simply accept the fact that you are accepted.*' If that happens to us we experience grace.
>
> (Tillich 1949: 163)

Tillich is not alone in seeing acceptance as much more than a therapeutic technique. In *Kerygma and Counseling* (1966), Tom Oden also explores the analogy between the acceptance inherent in a good counselling relationship and the divine acceptance that lies at the heart of evangelical theology. He argues that Karl Barth, whose evangelical theology underpins the proclamatory model outlined above, and Carl Rogers are not as far apart as might at first appear. Both are concerned with human self-actualization. Barth insists as strongly as Rogers that 'Man is summoned to be himself' (Barth 1961: 385; Rogers 1961: 163). Yet while both Barth and Rogers make use of the concept of self-actualization, there are significant differences in their understanding of that concept. Barth understands the self in terms of the so-called 'analogy of faith'. The self we are called to become is the self who has been created, judged and redeemed by God in Jesus Christ. Barth is saying that men and women can experience acceptance at a human level because in the events surrounding the life and death of Jesus Christ, God has declared himself to be One who accepts them unconditionally. For Rogers, self-realization is expressed in terms more purely humanistic:

> The characteristic movement, I have said, is for the client to permit himself to be the changing, fluid, process which he is . . . It means that as he moves towards acceptance of the 'is-ness' of himself, he accepts others increasingly in the same, listening, understanding way . . . It is to feel a growing pride in being a sensitive, open, realistic, inner-directed member of the human species.
>
> (Rogers 1961: 181)

In drawing parallels between the thought of Barth and Rogers, Oden is attempting to give a theological underpinning for good pastoral practice, demonstrating that therapeutic acceptance is not only analogous to the covenant relationship between God and man but is a manifestation of that relationship. While Barth's ideas are expressed in the language of Swiss Reformed theology, Oden's statement of his own central thesis gives his argument a wider relevance:

> There is a tacit ontological assumption of all effective therapy not that it is merely the counselor who accepts the client but that the client is acceptable as a human being by the ground of being itself, and that the final reality we confront in life is for us – Deus pro nobis.
>
> (Oden 1966: 21)

If acceptance is something more than a technique, if indeed the reality of human acceptance is the embodiment of the truth about an accepting God, then acceptance is not something 'done to' a client by a counsellor. Tillich understands that counsellors can only be accepting in their relationships with clients when they themselves have experienced acceptance at the deepest level in their own lives:

> The first aim, and in some sense the total aim, toward which we have to work in pastoral care is acceptance . . . The power which makes acceptance possible is the resource in all pastoral care. It must be effective in him who helps, and it must become effective in him who is helped . . . It is not as though the helper

was first helped some time ago and now can help himself, but that in the best act of helping, he is continuously helped himself. This means that both the pastor and the counsellee, the psychotherapist and the patient, are under the power of something which transcends both of them.

(Tillich 1959: 24)

For Tillich, pastoral care is only possible when both helper and helped have experience of acceptance in the name of a power which transcended them both. While Tillich points to the reality of the power of the 'New Being', he cautions against a too-easy use of traditional religious language in pastoral counselling. He believes that the language of depth psychology and existentialism are a form of 'providential support' for the pastoral counsellor. Tillich's main contribution is to provide, in his existential theology, a language and a set of concepts which can form a bridge between the pastoral counsellors and the secular therapists.

The first two metaphors of pastoral counselling I have outlined are those of the preacher and the healer. Counselling as proclamation has obvious limitations but it is in the process of transformation and it gives way to a different model in which meaning is allowed to emerge from the pastoral conversation. Instead of impregnating the client's story with meaning, the counsellor becomes a kind of midwife, standing by and giving support as meaning struggles to be born during the labour of counselling.

The metaphor of pastoral counselling as therapy also has its limitations. Counsellors are not medical doctors with drugs or any other quick fix to 'make things better'. Counsellors are at best 'wounded healers', people who themselves have experienced pain and suffering and yet have survived – and more. Through an acceptance of their own acceptance and a deeper appreciation of the ambiguous meaning of their own stories, they are enabled to accept other people and to stay with the pain as others share their stories. Being on a journey themselves, counsellors are equipped to walk alongside others for a while. From this there emerge two further metaphors for pastoral counselling.

Pastoral counselling as story-telling

Pastoral care involves assisting persons to move from talking generally about themselves and specifically about their problems to talking specifically about themselves and generally about their problems.

(Patton 1990: 894)

With these words, John Patton asserts that a major pastoral task is to assist counsellees to talk concretely about themselves and to discover some of the symbols, stories and myths of their lives. This proposal is in line with recent theological understandings of the pastoral task. New insights have emerged from the interaction between a development known as 'Narrative Theology' and pastoral counselling. In reaction against a view that sees truth as being conveyed only through abstract propositional statements, narrative theology is concerned to find personal meaning in stories and in the insights arising from them. We have already noted Stephen Crites' thesis that all experience has a narrative quality, and that meaning is generated in the interaction between the stories of our own lives and the sacred stories of our culture. A rediscovery of the importance of narrative and of its interpretation has provided a rationale for enabling people to understand the stories of their own lives. The discipline of hermeneutics is concerned with the principles of interpretation, particularly of written texts, and a new 'hermeneutical' approach to pastoral counselling has been developed in recent years. In the title of his book *The Living Human Document: Re-Visioning Pastoral Counseling in a Hermeneutic Mode* (1984), Charles Gerkin recaptures the words of Anton Boisen that there is no better library for understanding people than the 'living human documents' of people in crises. The task of pastoral counselling is to facilitate the interpretation and the reinterpretation of stories:

> To seek counseling sometimes means to seek an ally who will confirm one's own interpretation of experience as over against another interpretation insisted upon by another person whose interpretations carry weight with the seeker. For these, and other complex reasons the one seeking counseling comes asking for a fresh interpretation of what has been experienced, a new 'story' for his or her life.
>
> (Gerkin 1984: 26)

Yet the pastoral counsellor is not one who can simply provide an interpretation of the experience of another, because as well as being a listener to stories, the pastoral counsellor is also the bearer of stories – and a Story. Counsellors come with their own experience of life and their own interpretation of that experience. For this reason:

> Pastoral counselling may thus be understood as a dialogical hermeneutical process involving the counselor and counselee in communication across the boundaries of language worlds.
>
> (Gerkin 1984: 28)

We see again something of the mutuality involved in pastoral counselling. While it is not the task of counsellors to offer easy interpretations of the stories of their clients, neither dare they forget that they bring to the counselling relationship their own personal stories and their interpretations of them. Further, as I noted earlier in this chapter, the counsellor may be perceived as the bearer of another Story, a religious Story. Part of the task of pastoral counselling may be to explore the significance for the client of that Story and what light it shines upon his or her own.

As I have previously indicated, every community of faith has its 'big stories' which shape the cultural values and individual perceptions of its members. While affirming the importance of these stories in the lives of others, I must also recognize that, brought up within the Christian tradition, I can only speak with personal knowledge of the way in which the Christian story may function in the pastoral relationship. In the pastoral and spiritual context that story is often part of the common heritage of counsellor and counsellee. If Stephen Crites is right, that our consciousness is formed as we mediate between the mundane stories of our lives and the sacred stories of our culture, then we should not be surprised if the Christian story at least contributes to a reinterpretation of the client's story. We should not be surprised if, in the recollection of stories about death and resurrection, clients find a hint of comfort in the midst of loss; nor should we cease to expect that stories of personal commitment will inspire the precarious vision that underlies the rediscovery of personal meaning; nor that the personal acceptance experienced in a counselling relationship located within a community of faith is seen to be the human expression of a story whose central theme is unconditional grace and the possibility of new beginnings. What is important is that interpretations are not imposed but allowed to emerge from the stories inherent in the counselling process. Pastoral counselling can be characterized by a *freedom* to allow the 'big story' (be it Christian or some other) to be part of the intercourse of narratives from which meaning is born. In this respect it differs from other religiously orientated forms of counselling which sometimes seem to be driven by a *compulsion* to tell the 'big story', a compulsion rooted more in the needs of the counsellor than in those of the counsellee.

It may well be that in the awareness of this process there is something of value for counselling in other contexts. In every context, clients come with stories, each with their own nuances and their own meanings. To every counselling situation, counsellors bring the stories of their own lives and the values which have shaped them. It is as inappropriate in secular counselling as it is in pastoral counselling that the beliefs and values of the counsellor should be imposed upon the client. But it is equally necessary to be aware of the beliefs and values which both client and counsellor bring to their relationship. The possibility of value-free counselling is the biggest myth of all! It is not to be expected that everyone will share a common view of the sacred stories and myths that shape the context of pastoral counselling. What might be hoped is that counselling in the pastoral context may be seen as a paradigm for counselling in other contexts. The values, personal stories and cultural myths which permeate counselling in every context could then be acknowledged and freely explored as they either inhibit or contribute to the therapeutic process.

Pastoral counselling as companionship

In *Rediscovering Pastoral Care* (1986) Alastair Campbell explores the metaphor of pastoral care as companionship on a journey:

> Companions are more than chance acquaintances. They interrupt their own preoccupations and pitch in their lot with others. Perhaps the companionship only lasts for a short space of time, but while it lasts the companion *shares* with the other . . . We can only share in someone else's life search if we are prepared to expose ourselves a little, speaking about things which matter deeply to us as well as the other and risking ourselves in the service of the other. But our companionship fails if our words dominate *the other's* search, or if our actions remove *the other's* need to journey on.
>
> (Campbell 1986: 92)

This metaphor is far removed from that of 'the expert' counsellor who maintains a clinical detachment from the client. For the carer it involves mutuality and personal exposure and risk although obviously not to the point where the counsellor unloads a personal agenda upon a client. For this to happen carers must be aware of where they are in their own journeys and life-searches. It is at this point that the boundaries between pastoral counselling and spiritual direction become somewhat blurred, particularly with regard to those contemporary forms of spiritual direction whose emphasis lies more in accompanying people on their personal journeys rather than 'directing' them.

Of relevance to this metaphor of pastoral counselling as companionship on a journey is recent work on faith development. Various attempts have been made to systematize the different dimensions of human growth and development. Freud (1905) wrote of various aspects of emotional and sexual development; Piaget (1950) proposed a model for the development of cognitive thinking in children; Erikson (1965) developed a model of psychosocial development which he called 'The Eight Ages of Man'; and Kohlberg (1976) researched the development of moral thinking. Work on faith development has been pioneered by Fowler (1981) who identifies seven 'stages of faith'. These are (a) *Primal faith* (infancy) in which are sown the seeds of trust and mistrust; (b) *Intuitive-projective faith* (2–6 years) in which children's capacities for attention to mystery and the numinous are formed by their perceptions of adults' convictions; (c) *Mythic-literal faith* (7–12 years) in which, through a firm grasp of cause and effect, children challenge their previous perceptions and find meanings through narrative and story, their interpretations, albeit, tending to be fairly literal; (d) *Synthetic-conventional faith* (12–17 years) in which the young person begins to construct an image of the self and to work at a unifying set of attitudes, beliefs and values which will establish an identity with his or her peers; (e) *Individuative-reflective faith* (17–35 years) in which people move on from being dependent on the views of others to a more self-reflective awareness with a sense of autonomy and in which the inner meanings of stories and symbols can be stated in conceptual terms; (f) *Conjunctive faith* (35 years–) involving the ability to tolerate polarity and ambiguity, together with a humility that avoids ideological overconfidence and an awareness of the inadequacy of all human effort to grasp the reality of Being; and (g) *Universalizing faith,* according to Fowler a rare stage which only a few attain, characterized by a lack of concern for the self and by a love for others grounded in the Being of God.

This framework is helpful in allowing counsellors to 'place' clients in terms of their religious development. It should be noted, however, that the ages at which these transitions are reckoned to take place should be treated with considerable caution. Indeed, in the process of normal development, it is possible for people to become 'stuck' at one particular stage of faith development and never to move on. As I write, there is much controversy among Christians over the remarks of the Bishop of Durham concerning the literal truth of the stories of the Virgin Birth of Jesus Christ. One way of understanding the deep feelings aroused (but not the only one, for there are profound theological issues as well) is to see the issue in terms of faith-development theory. Those whose faith is at the Mythic-literal level will wish to hold to the literal truth of the Bible stories, while those at the Individuative-reflective level are able to see a deeper meaning of such stories which is not dependent upon their literal truth. If Scott Peck (1987: 195) is right in his observation that people who differ by more than one stage in their faith development find it almost impossible to communicate with one another, then it is not difficult for us to understand why there is so much mutual incomprehension of the different positions held.

In a later book, Fowler (1987) explores the relationship between faith development and pastoral care. In any congregation, that ministry is exercised with a group of people at very different stages in their faith development, each with very different needs. These needs are complicated by the changes that people experience in their lives whether these changes are necessary because of normal development or in working out the implications of personal choices or in coming to terms with intrusive events that change the course of human lives. It is important to note that Fowler is saying nothing about the *content* of people's faith but rather about the way in which faith or belief systems function under certain circumstances. Thus, although Fowler writes from firmly within the Christian tradition, the theory is of wider application to the understanding of adherents of other religious traditions and even to those who profess no religious faith but who still (inevitably) have a set of beliefs about the world.

While Fowler's work has been of great value, it has not been free from criticism, albeit of a constructive nature. Jacobs (1988) attempts to bring into relationship to one another all the various developmental theories listed above. However, in a subsequent publication, essentially a complete reworking of the material in that book, Jacobs (1993a), while reaffirming his indebtedness to Fowler, diverges from this model in three significant ways. First, he questions the whole concept of linearity or 'stages' espoused by Fowler, preferring to base his developmental theory on the more complex 'metro map' of religious and philosophical belief proposed by the British theologian Don Cupitt (1986). Second, Jacobs extends this model to other forms of belief besides faith itself. Third, he questions the usefulness of the last of Fowler's stages, viewing it not as a separate stage to be attained by only a few but as a more intense form of the level of faith described by Fowler's penultimate stage (Conjunctive faith) and experienced, from time to time, by many. One of the 'elect' whom Fowler did give as an example of his final stage (Universalizing faith) was Thomas Merton, a Catholic monk who has made a deep impact on contemporary understanding of Christian spirituality. Jacobs (1993a: 167) points out that despite this deep spirituality, Merton was not entirely free from self-centredness.

Be that as it may, his writings have been of profound influence. While he did not write specifically about psychotherapy, I now wish to argue that in the story of Merton's own journey there is a way of transcending the apparent splitting between secular psychotherapy and religious faith within pastoral counselling.

In *The Seven Storey Mountain* (1948), Merton describes the early part of his journey which includes the story of his conversion from being a dissolute young man in the New York of the 1930s to becoming a Catholic of the most traditional kind, and then his entry into the monastery at Gethsemani, Kentucky. His later life and writings take a surprising turn, for if his early writings describe his turning away from the world, his later work displays a conversion back to the world, as it were. Not that he left the monastery (at least not until near the end of his life), but from his cloistered existence he made an impact upon the American civil-rights movement, the protests against the war in Vietnam, ecumenical relationships between Christian churches and interfaith dialogue with non-Christian religions. It was as though the more deeply he entered into his spiritual journey, the more open he became towards the world. His search for a relevant spirituality and his search for what is most authentically human became one and the same. Does Merton's spiritual journey not have implications for our understanding of pastoral counselling?

Merton's own journey recapitulates some of the theological trends of recent decades. An early liberalism accommodating itself to the dominant secularity of the age is followed by a conservative reaction which in turn gives way to the search for a different kind of spirituality, one which encounters God not in religion as such, but in the suffering and striving of the world. Within the development of counselling in the pastoral and spiritual context, I have already noted the first two of these phases. The growth of a pastoral counselling dominated by the secular therapies has been followed by the resurgence of more conservative approaches of the so-called 'Christian counsellors'. I believe that in the spirituality of Merton there are insights that enable pastoral counselling to transcend these polarities. One Merton scholar has written:

The early Merton seemed obsessed with religious questions, and the word 'salvation' had to do with saving one's soul. But the later and more mature Merton realised that salvation was the therapeutic wholeness which was God's love and grace invading the human life at every level. The more he experienced the forgiveness and the loving embrace of God, the more he felt the questions, the problems, the agony of human existence in the world. He is adamantly opposed to those who have never felt high ecstasy or black despair, but who smilingly concoct smooth religious answers or formulate firm, dogmatic propositions or answers to the agony and absurdity felt by men of integrity who recognise the human dilemma of contemporary existence.

(Ramon 1989: 85)

'Salvation as therapeutic wholeness' . . . 'God's love and grace invading the human life at every level'. The paradox at the heart of Merton's spirituality is the same paradox that lies at the heart of pastoral counselling, a paradox that holds in creative tension both congruence with the Christian story and the insights of secular psychotherapy. The paradox is that the search for an authentic spirituality sets us free from the bondage of religion. Set free from the *compulsion* to talk about God, there is a new and deeper freedom to talk about God and *not* to talk about God. There is a 'time to speak and a time to keep silence' (Eccles 3: 7). With Merton, we can affirm that 'salvation is the therapeutic wholeness which is God's love invading the human life at every level'. When people in emotional or spiritual distress see the way forward on their journey, then we can celebrate the presence of God, free from the compulsion to clothe the process in religious language. There is a time to be silent . . . but there is also a time to speak. In his search for that which was most truly human, in his work for civil rights, in his dialogue with Christians who were not Catholics and with monks who were not Christian, Merton did not cease to be who he was: a Christian, a Catholic, a monk and a priest. His spiritual, world-affirming journey did not deny that identity. In its engagement with the secular psychotherapies, neither does pastoral counselling need to lose its Christian identity as care offered in the context of a community of faith. Set free from the compulsion to be 'religious', it has a genuine freedom to point beyond the secular to the One who is the source of all healing. It may well be that the distinctive contribution of pastoral counselling to caring for people lies in a discerning use of this freedom.

· FIVE ·

Professional relationships in counselling in the pastoral and spiritual context

Those who counsel in this context may be considered part of a large network which encompasses many in the mainline Christian churches and beyond them, often in other religious traditions and sometimes in none. In this chapter, I explore the professional relationships of the network of pastoral care, not only between that network and other professional groups but within the network itself.

RELATIONSHIPS WITH PROFESSIONALS IN OTHER DISCIPLINES

Before we consider the relationship of those who counsel in the pastoral and spiritual context to the wider community of care and support, there is a fundamental question to be addressed. How appropriate is it to speak of professionalism in this context?

The *Dictionary of Pastoral Care and Counseling* defines 'Professionalism' as follows:

> A profession is a calling, vocation or employment that requires specialized knowledge and skills, is characterized by and conforms to technical and ethical procedures and standards that have been established by a group of peer professionals, and is both the principal occupation and source of financial gain to those who practice it.
>
> (Murphy 1990: 959)

Traditionally, the ordained ministry has been regarded as one of the learned professions along with medicine, education and law. It could be argued that the ordained ministry itself fits the above definition of 'profession' very well. Generally speaking, however, pastoral counselling is neither the principal occupation of the clergy nor their main source of financial gain. There are, in fact, very few 'professional' pastoral counsellors in Britain in the sense that pastoral counselling provides a substantial proportion of their income. There are also, however, in private practice, a number who profess a spiritual component in their counselling model. In this respect, Britain differs significantly from North America where many members of the American Association of Pastoral Counselors (who are invariably clergy) earn their livelihood in church-related counselling centres. Further, many of those in Britain who train as counsellors and subsequently offer their services in counselling centres set up by church bodies are lay people who receive no payment for their work.

In recent times there have been those who have sought to distance ministry from some of the negative aspects of 'professionalism'. A specifically British contribution to debate about the nature of pastoral care and counselling has been to challenge the appropriateness of an emerging professional model. We have already noted the plea of the late Bob Lambourne that pastoral counselling in Britain should not be 'professional . . . standardised, defined' but 'lay, corporate, adventurous, variegated and diffuse' (Lambourne 1971: 26) (see page 28).

Alastair Campbell has also written of 'The Professional Captivity of Pastoral Care' (1985), expressing certain reservations about the notion of professionalism in pastoral care. He argues that it leads to a denial of the mutuality that is inherent in all *pastoral* relationships; that the imbalance of power which characterized professional relationships is inappropriate in the pastoral context; that the historic notion of 'learned' professions encouraged an intellectualism which does not necessarily fit well with (in his case) a Christian ministry of love; that a professional model of counselling can be too concerned with personal adjustment and fulfilment divorced from any ethical or political context; and, finally, that professionalism is not only individualistic, it is change-resistant, conservative of existing social structures (Campbell 1985: 40–7).

Campbell's anxieties about the balance of power in pastoral relationships find an echo in the work of other counsellors who profess to take seriously the spiritual dimension of human experience. Thus Brian Thorne writing from a person-centred perspective emphasizes:

the importance of rejecting the pursuit of control or authority over other persons . . . In the counselling relationship this implies an ever-watchful attentiveness to any imbalance in power between counsellor and client and a constant seeking to equalise power through any procedures, whether verbal or otherwise, which remedy a power imbalance.

(Thorne 1991: 172)

While there are legitimate anxieties about a model of pastoral counselling which is over-professionalized, there is another sense in which pastoral counsellors must be thoroughly professional in their approach if they are to achieve credibility. There is an appropriate professionalism required in pastoral counselling in that it is (or ought to be) 'a calling characterized by conformity to technical and ethical procedures and standards that have been established by a group of peer professionals' (Murphy 1990: 959). Indeed, it can be argued that the pastoral counselling movement has been leading the way in setting standards and establishing codes of professional conduct for ministry. At the time of writing, the Association for Pastoral Care and Counselling is in the process of hosting a series of consultations to discuss the value and quality of pastoral work (Foskett 1993: 25). These developments can only lead to ministry generally being set on a more professional footing. The importance of this cannot be overestimated. The extent to which counsellors in this context can enjoy fruitful co-operation with other professionals depends on the extent to which they are perceived by others – and themselves – as 'professional' in the best sense of the word.

Interdisciplinary relationships

As a hospital chaplain, I observed that when doctors referred patients and their families to organizations like Cruse or the Marriage Counselling Service or Alcoholics Anonymous, they did so because there was a clear perception of the ethos and standards of these organizations. Sometimes, members of other professions find it difficult to form a clear perception of counselling in the pastoral context partly because, as I have argued, it is such a diverse activity giving expression to many different religious and psychological understandings. Stereotyping can also be a problem, on occasion as big a problem as a lack of clear perceptions.

On one occasion, three divinity students were about to begin a hospital placement at the same time as three social-work students. At an early point in their time with us, my colleague, the social-work teacher, and I decided to set up a joint exercise. Before the two groups of students met one another, we asked each to produce some kind of picture that illustrated their understanding of the other profession. The divinity students produced a drawing of a young woman wearing a T-shirt and torn jeans, carrying a banner with slogans protesting against the injustices of the world. The social-work students drew a sketch of an old man, dressed in black, carrying a Bible and preaching against sin. When the two groups met, it turned out that the social workers were mainly mature women wearing skirts and blouses, more interested in counselling than revolution; it was the divinity students who turned up casually dressed espousing political views much more radical than those of the social-work students!

Sometimes, we *think* we know about other professionals, what they are like and how they function and it is only experience that breaks down prejudices. I think that for most of the time I enjoyed good relationships with my social-work colleagues, but we had to keep on working at it. If truth were told, I was a little in awe of them, at least to begin with. They, so I thought, were the real professionals, they were properly trained as counsellors (an assumption I later found to be false), they had free access to the patients' case-notes. I also found that they looked askance at what I was about. How did I use my freedom to wander around the hospital and speak to everybody? Did I try to convert patients? Or did I 'upset' them by praying over them?

Stereotyping becomes a problem when attitudes are projected on to individuals and organizations that owe more to the past experience or the inner world of someone who is thinking of making a referral than to reality. Nowhere is this factor more potent than in situations with an ethical dimension. Stereotyping may inhibit the referral of clients by social workers (or of patients by doctors) to pastors or pastoral counsellors because of what are imagined to be the judgemental attitudes of the latter group. On such matters as abortion, homosexuality or cohabitation there may be a perceived lack of sympathy on the part of those who counsel in a religious context. Indeed, the problem may not always be a stereotype but a real one. The fact is that within religious communities there are profound differences of opinion and feeling on social issues, especially in relation to sexuality.

There is in fact sometimes greater polarization within religious communities than there is between these communities and the secular world. On the abortion issue, there are few in the churches who consider the termination of a pregnancy to be other than an occasion for sadness. Polarization exists, however, between those who condemn abortion under any circumstances (largely Roman Catholics and conservative evangelicals) and those who consider that abortion is permissible under certain conditions, with opinion varying as to the relative weight that should be given to medical and social factors. On the matter of homosexuality, again there are profound emotive divisions within the churches. On the one hand, there are those who hold that scripture condemns homosexuality and that the only role for the Church is to facilitate repentance and change; on the other hand there are those who believe that the tradition has to be interpreted in the light of new insights from psychodynamic and genetic studies.

Strongly held ethical views cannot but influence the practice of counselling in contexts where they are held to be important. Because of the widely shared perception that the Church is anti-sex (not entirely undeserved), it is unlikely that people with a sexual problem will seek help from the Church unless they are sure that they will not be judged and found wanting.

This wide difference in ethical stances can also make it difficult for other professions to refer their clients or patients to counsellors in the pastoral field. It is for this very reason that when referrals are made from outside the context, it is often done on the basis of a knowledge of the pastor or counsellor as a person and not because of their role or position.

As time went by in the hospital I began to be asked to see particular patients or their families, but generally these referrals came from staff with whom I had already established a good working relationship. One evening I was called into the hospital to see the parents of a very sick child. When I arrived at the duty room, the ward sister gave me a rapid resumé of the situation and rushed out of the room. As she left, she poked her head back around the door and said 'Oh, David, when I asked if they would like to see the chaplain, they wanted to know if you were a Christian.' And off she rushed again. I appreciated the sensitivity of this referral. The ward sister made me aware that this anxious couple would be looking for a particular kind of Christian ministry. I suspect, however, that the referral would not have been made in exactly these terms without my previous involvement with both patients and staff in that ward.

If other professions have problems in referring clients to pastoral counsellors, the movement in the opposite direction also has its complications. It is possible for ministers of local congregations to err in two diametrically opposed ways. On the one hand, there are some clergy who never refer at all. Some ministers believe they ought to be able to cope with every problem they encounter in their parishes; some indeed may fail to be aware that a problem exists. Others are hesitant about referral to a secular therapist for fear that the faith of their parishioners will be undermined. On the other hand, there are others, perhaps a smaller number, who refer too quickly, lacking confidence in the effectiveness of their own ministry. Sometimes (as we noted in Switzer's response to Krebs in Chapter Three), there are people who are not ill but who, as they go through a bad patch in their lives, can benefit from the kind of support that is best given by a minister who is prepared to listen to them.

Skill in referral is very important. Sometimes it is the clergy who first become aware that something is wrong with a parishioner. Good pastors are sensitive at the margins where normal grief verges on the pathological; they may be admitted into the secret pain of a woman coping with an alcoholic husband; or they may be allowed a glimpse of the suffering behind the façade of an apparently good marriage. Such discoveries or revelations should at least cause a minister to consider whether he or she is the best person to help, or whether an attempt should be made to enable those who suffer to draw upon the resources of others more skilled. It is often the task of the clergy to encourage people to seek help but without giving them the impression that they are being abandoned pastorally. There is an art in referring parishioners for more skilled help than a minister can provide, and doing so in such a way that support and encouragement continues to be given, without meddling in the therapeutic process.

'I must see a **Christian** counsellor'

Reference has already been made to the fact that ministers may hesitate to refer parishioners to secular counselling agencies out of a fear that psychotherapy may damage their faith. The same kind of resistance may be demonstrated by religious people themselves. This issue has been perceptively explored by David Mumford, who is both a psychiatrist and a non-stipendiary minister of the Church of England. In an article called 'May I See a *Christian* Psychiatrist?' (1987), Mumford explores the fantasies and fears which may lie behind such a request. There are fantasies relating both to the power and the powerlessness of the psychiatrist. On the one hand, the psychiatrist may be perceived as having the ability to read a person's mind without the patient intending to give away any secrets, as having the power to heal or destroy; on the other hand, particularly among depressed patients, there may be a fantasy that the psychiatrist is powerless to help (a view almost certainly not shared by the psychiatrist). There are also realistic fears, particularly when the patient is about to meet an unknown doctor within the National Health Service, especially when many psychiatrists are assumed to be dismissive of religion.

> Will I be taken seriously as a religious person? My religion is important to me; will the psychiatrist see that and respect that? Will I be *understood* as a religious person? Or will the religious side of me be ignored, discounted or undermined?
>
> (Mumford 1987: 20)

From the point of view of the psychiatrist the deeply held convictions and religious language of some patients may be seen as part of their problem. Such defences against unpleasant feelings can only be overcome where the patient is highly motivated to change and where great patience and endurance is shown by the psychiatrist. The possibility of manipulation by some religious patients makes psychiatrists wary of disclosing their own religious beliefs. Nevertheless, Mumford stresses the need for psychiatrists to be aware of their own beliefs (whether religious or anti-religious) with the proviso that they should be able to bracket these for the period of the consultation, attempting to understand the patient in the patient's own terms, without imposing value judgements.

Mumford's comments are also relevant when potential clients make a specific request to be referred to a Christian counsellor. On the one hand, we can sympathize with religious people who wish to have their faith taken seriously and who are afraid that it will be undermined by a secular counsellor (although this may be another example of stereotyping). On the other hand, Christian counsellors, and indeed any who counsel in the pastoral and spiritual context, must be aware of the unreal, sometimes even magical, expectations which may lie behind such a request. Psychiatrists are free to decide to reveal nothing of their own beliefs. For reasons which I discussed in Chapter Four, this is not normally an option for counsellors in the pastoral and spiritual context. It may therefore be important that clear contracts or shared expectations between counsellors and clients are established at an early stage in order to avoid misunderstanding.

RELATIONSHIPS BETWEEN COUNSELLORS OF DIFFERENT FAITHS

Sometimes professional relationships between counsellors working in different religious traditions can be more relaxed than among those working within the same tradition. For example, there has been growing appreciation of the Jewish contribution to what has been a predominantly Christian movement. In Chapter One, where I described the growth of pastoral counselling in Britain, I drew attention to the fact that Irene Bloomfield and Rabbi Danny Smith, who were instrumental in the foundation of the Jewish Raphael Counselling Centre, were early participants in the work of the Roman Catholic Dympna Centre. Within the European and International pastoral care movements there have always been a small number of Jews who have made a contribution to these organizations out of all proportion to their numbers. It is perhaps because of these contributions that when the constitution of the International Council on Pastoral Care and Counselling was drawn up, those deemed eligible for membership were 'Organizations or individuals who have an active involvement in the practice and/or teaching of pastoral care and counselling *within the Jewish and Christian traditions*' (my italics). Looking back over several meetings of the Council, I can recall many occasions when we had to work hard to understand how our cultural backgrounds influenced our differences of approach to certain matters. I cannot recall, however, any substantive issue when we split along specifically religious lines – apart from the place of services of worship in a conference programme.

How is it that counsellors within different religious traditions can find such a measure of agreement? Again I find some helpful insights in the writings of Thomas Merton. While remaining a deeply committed Catholic, Merton, especially towards the end of his life, experienced a deep sense of spiritual unity with Christians of other traditions and indeed with monks of the great Eastern religions. He writes:

> I will be a better Catholic, not if I can *refute* every shade of Protestantism, but if I can affirm the truth in it and still go further.
> So, too, with the Muslims, the Hindus, the Buddhists, etc. This does not mean syncretism, indifferentism, the vapid and careless friendliness that accepts everything by thinking of nothing. There is much that one cannot 'affirm', 'accept', but first one must say 'yes' where one really can.
> If I affirm myself as a Catholic, merely by denying all that is Muslim, Jewish, Protestant, Hindu, Buddhist, etc., in the end I will find that that there is not much left for me to affirm as a Catholic; and certainly no breath of the Spirit with which to affirm it.

(Merton 1968: 141)

One of Merton's biographers, Brother Ramon, points out (1989: 194) that for Merton, this attitude to people of other faiths, this openness to the truth of their beliefs that did not threaten his own, was only possible on the basis of a sense of personal integration and interior unity within the self. It would be presumptuous to claim that this quality of openness is held exclusively by trained counsellors. Put another way, however, there can be no effective counselling without this kind of openness to others; and an essential part of the process of becoming such a counsellor is to set out on the journey of personal integration and interior unity, the journey inwards, decribed by Dag Hammarskjold as 'the longest journey'. It would be a mistake to regard the ecumenism of the pastoral care movement as being based on the lowest common denominator of psychological reductionism. It is far deeper than that. It is based on an acceptance of the complexity of the inner lives and varieties of religious experience of men and women.

In Chapter Two I drew attention to the burgeoning New Age movement, a feature of which is a whole raft of alternative therapies. This, too, is a complex phenomenon. Entering a New Age bookshop, we may be met by the smell of incense, the sound of tinkling bells, the sight of scores of crystals – and find an excellent selection of books on counselling. Sometimes Christians are given to wholesale condemnation of the New Age movement, or worse still as labelling as 'New Age' (and therefore as 'bad') everything with which they disagree (even the books of Scott Peck). I confess there is much in the New Age movement that I personally find bizarre and unacceptable. Yet blanket condemnation of the movement does less than justice to important truths and may lead to the neglect of therapies that may be beneficial and integrated into counselling in this context. In 1993, the Church of Scotland produced a report on New Age phenomena. In seeking (rightly) to illustrate the diversity of this movement, it grouped together 'self-understanding through transpersonal psychology, getting in touch with your inner self, getting to know your spirit guides, and receiving spiritual guidance from whales, dolphins, extra-terrestrials, and even Barbie dolls' (1993b: 491). The all-embracing sweep of this statement, however, detracts from an earlier and more discerning one which recognizes that 'certain New Age techniques can be used beneficially within the concept and practice of Christianity'. If transpersonal psychology facilitates self-understanding, and if being in touch with our inner selves is a necessary precondition of effective counselling in any context, then these possible insights should be assessed and valued for what they are. They should not be rejected out of hand simply because they have been labelled 'New Age', nor found wanting because of alleged association with the weirder aspects of the movement.

Relationships between people of different religious faiths will always be fraught with difficulties and misunderstandings, from which counsellors in the pastoral and spiritual context are not immune. But perhaps counsellors in this context are at least equipped to understand the belief systems of those who differ from them, even where agreement is not possible. It is possible to accept people as human beings without accepting their beliefs.

RELATIONSHIPS WITH OTHER CLERGY

'There are varieties of service' (I Cor. 12, 5) wrote St Paul in the first century and his words are just as true today. There are varieties of ministry within the Church and not all of them would give a high priority to counselling. Besides the counsellors, there are social activists, evangelists and sacramentalists. Within a broad church, there is room for all provided there is mutual tolerance and acceptance if not agreement.

There has often been a polarization in the Church between the advocates of political involvement and the specialists in pastoral care. Lambourne (1970) identifies this problem in a personal impression of pastoral care in the United States:

> There seems to be a split, perhaps a growing split, between those who are teaching Practical Theology through pastoral counselling and clinical pastoral care (Group A) and those who are teaching it through field work in depressed urban settings (Group B). The former lean heavily, and sometimes exclusively, upon psychology. The latter lean heavily, and sometimes exclusively, on sociology. The former teach sensitivity by psychological interpretation in controlled unstructured groups, the latter by selected exposure to cultural shock.
>
> (Lambourne 1970: 133)

Social activists accuse the counsellors of a psychological quietism which tries to help people adjust to their problems while turning a blind eye to the social and political roots of these problems. Counsellors accuse the social activists of failing to understand both the inner motivations of people in public life and the depth of human suffering caused by social problems (and sometimes also by the proposed solutions). In the above article, Lambourne writes of 'the separation of the theory and the art of loving from the theory and

the art of justice'. Perhaps if the counsellors need a deeper awareness of sociological causes of human distress, the social activists
need to be more aware of the workings of the human psyche. In
the final chapter I shall try to show how attempts are being made
to address this issue in new approaches to pastoral education.

Differences between pastoral counsellors and social activists reflect a tension between psychological and sociopolitical emphases.
There can also be differences between pastoral counsellors and clergy
with a more overtly evangelical emphasis. I am not thinking here
of those trained as Christian counsellors who are trying to integrate
psychological insights with an evangelical understanding of ministry, but rather of clergy who reject *any* psychological understanding
of human personality, reducing all pastoral relationships to issues of
sin and repentance (or simply of 'common sense').

There are also significant differences between pastoral counsellors
and a third group of clergy involved in pastoral ministry. I refer to
those whose ministry is understood primarily in sacramental terms.
This was especially evident in hospital chaplaincy where what appeared to be most important for many of my Roman Catholic
colleagues, and for some of my Anglican ones, was to take Holy
Communion to patients. This is in no way to denigrate the importance of sacramental ministry in pastoral care. Indeed, I believe that
this is an emphasis which, within the Reformed tradition, we need
to recover. Sensitivity, however, is extremely important. Two very
different experiences spring to mind. In the first, after a pastoral
relationship lasting several months, I took communion one Sunday
to a devout Presbyterian lady who had a deep love of church music.
After I gave her communion in her hospital room, we listened
together to the last magnificent chorus of Bach's St Matthew Pas-
sion. She died peacefully two days later. In the second, I offered to
bring communion to a minister colleague facing major surgery. As
soon as the words were out of my mouth, I knew I had made a
mistake. The colour drained from his face and it was obvious that
he thought I was offering to bring him the last rites. Notwithstanding, I believe that we must continue to explore the interaction of
what are often considered to be separate ministries. Each needs the
other. A purely sacramental ministry can miss an understanding of
the interpersonal and psychodynamic factors in a pastoral relationship. A pastoral relationship shaped entirely by the philosophy and
techniques of the secular therapies may fail to draw on rich spiritual
resources.

Why is it that some clergy see their ministry shaped by the counselling paradigm while others emphatically do not? We have already

noted at the conclusion of Chapter Two that many people become counsellors because they themselves have been through a particularly difficult time in their own lives and have been helped by counselling. There is also research that indicates the existence of a 'helping personality' (Eadie 1975), a personality pattern common among many members of the so-called caring professions including the clergy. The Myers-Briggs Type Indicator, based on Jung's theory of personality types (see p. 10), identifies four different human temperaments. One of these four groups, which is found in only twelve per cent of the general population, constitutes half the mainline Protestant clergy. This group, the 'Authenticity-Seeking, Relationship-Oriented' pastors:

> bring a natural skill to pastoral counselling as they are deeply in tune with people. They quickly experience empathy with parishioners and readily become deeply involved . . . They may be less competent when a parishioner merely wants practical help; they will try to push for the deeper issues involved. They are best when working with parishioners' values, emotions and interpersonal problems.
>
> (Oswald and Kroeger 1988: 86)

The other three groups have been designated the 'Action-Oriented' pastors (interested in practical problem-solving), the 'Intellectual, Competence-Seeking' pastors (fascinated by intellectual ideas), and 'Conserving-Serving, Serving' pastors (committed to the maintenance of worthwhile institutions). While the Myers-Briggs Type Indicator does not explain *why* these four temperaments exist, the theory does help to explain why those involved in different kinds of ministry sometimes find it difficult to understand one another. They also provide a vehicle which can facilitate better communication between people of different temperaments – including clergy who enjoy counselling and clergy who do not.

Clergy as clients

A further important aspect of the relationship between pastoral counsellors and other clergy arises when clergy themselves become clients. Most ministers are involved in some kind of pastoral care, whether offering the gift of friendship to parishioners or involving sophisticated counselling techniques. Pastoral care is usually only one facet of a very diverse ministry which makes a variety of demands on clergy. These demands can reflect the expectations of parishioners or of the clergy themselves, and they may not be realizable because of the constraints of time or skill. It should not surprise us therefore that, from time to time, ministers themselves experience a need for counselling. Counselling for the clergy themselves may, therefore, enhance the contribution of a significant group of workers in this context. I now examine (a) the pastoral needs of ministers; (b) research into the nature of the problem; and (c) some contemporary responses to these needs.

The pastoral needs of ministers

Throughout the caring professions there is widespread concern about the phenomenon of 'burnout'. The ordained ministry has not been exempt from this concern. 'Burnout' has been defined as:

> A syndrome, often occurring among individuals in helping professions, involving emotional and physical exhaustion, depersonalisation, and a feeling of reduced personal accomplishment.
> (Congo 1990: 112)

Research is now available demonstrating that within all the major denominations ministers are experiencing some degree of personal stress. Irvine (1989) undertook a survey of isolation in a random sample of two hundred parish ministers in the Church of Scotland. A response of nearly eighty per cent indicated that isolation was evident in three primary areas: (1) **professional isolation**: facing on a daily basis all the pressures of ministry without support either from colleagues in ministry or from other professionals in the community; (2) **social isolation**: meeting other people solely as 'the minister' without other significant human interaction; and (3) **spiritual isolation**: lacking others who would minister to them, bringing to them the comfort and grace they try to bring to others. Many ministers could not identify a pastor to whom they would turn for spiritual guidance. Isolation among the clergy is not primarily a geographical problem; from a social-psychological perspective a minister can feel isolated in a large city.

Fletcher (1990) has published the results of two studies of Church of England clergy, the first a general survey of two hundred and thirty priests (a sixty-two per cent response) and the second a study of three hundred and ninety homosexual clergy. In relation to the general survey he comments:

> Many aspects of work were associated with experienced strain, and job demands and job disillusionment in particular seemed to play a role in depression and general anxiety. The job demands

related to having to put on a public face; the lack of tangible results and being in conflict situations were significant in this respect, although those with the highest level of strain showed different perceptions on many different work factors compared to the clergy with lower levels of strain.

Overall, however, the objective measure of strain showed the clergy to be under less stress than one might expect.

(Fletcher 1990: 44)

Fletcher's second study reveals that among homosexual clergy stress levels are very high:

The levels of anxiety, depression and physical manifestations of stress are a major cause for concern. While it appeared from the study of parochial clergy . . . that clergy in general have quite low levels of strain, the homosexual clergy showed disturbingly high levels; as many as 34 per cent of clergy in some parish locations were significantly depressed.

(Fletcher 1990: 84)

The extent to which the ordained ministry experience work-related stress is difficult to quantify. What is certain is that in almost all the main denominations it is perceived to be a problem. And irrespective of its extent, there can be little doubt of the depth of the distress experienced by some individuals. Nor should it be forgotten that when men and women become ministers they do not cease to be subject to the same vicissitudes and vulnerabilities as the rest of the human race. Indeed, the fact that they are ministers may make it harder for them to find help, because of the expectation on the part of others – and sometimes of themselves – that they, of all people, ought to be able to cope. I now examine some theories which attempt to explain why being a minister is a source of stress.

Why ministry induces stress

There are two main approaches seeking to explain the phenomenon of burnout in ministry. The first locates the problems within the circumstances of contemporary ministry, i.e. in the external world of the minister; the second identifies the existence of a particular kind of personality pattern in the clergy, i.e. within the inner world of the minister.

External factors which contribute to ministerial stress have been related to role conflict and role confusion (Winton and Cameron 1986). Sometimes the role expectations of ministers are not congruent

with those of their parishioners (who may themselves have widely
conflicting expectations of their ministers). There are also particular
pressures on clergy marriages. Martin (1986) identifies two of these.
Normally ministers live in tied houses. While manses and vicarages
have their advantages (mostly for the congregations), they can
engender a sense of insecurity among the clergy and their families.
They are also, in a sense, 'public' houses which can lead to the feeling of living in a gold-fish bowl. Martin also identifies the importance of the minister's symbolic role. A minister may go along with
the expectations of some parishioners that he will be pastorally
available at all times, leading to an inability to plan regular time
with spouse and family. This 'affair' with the Church is one many
spouses find difficult to fight. The expectations of congregations,
real or imagined, through either conflict or collusion with them,
can also lead to health problems:

> For instance one priest saw the expectations of the parish as
> being quite onerous; he felt he had to be reliable, a hard worker,
> consistent, holy, contemporary, a regular visitor of the elderly,
> a person containing all the great virtues. He went on to talk
> about 'being taken over by other forces outside myself', of
> people making continuous demands on him and of knowing
> no way to respond to them. The study where he continued to
> work became his refuge away from people. People were de-
> manding beings who attacked him. The anger he felt took on
> physical symptoms and the family fragmented.
>
> (Martin 1986: 15)

This particular account of clergy breakdown would lead one to
suspect that it was not simply 'other forces' outside the self which
were at work. In a major study on the health of ministers of the
Church of Scotland, Eadie (1972, 1973) found that stress did make
a significant contribution to illness and disintegration in the experience of Scottish clergy, and that a variety of external circumstances certainly contributed to that stress. However, 'while the
external pressures were real enough, what matters is the way in
which the clergyman perceives and responds to such conditions'
(Eadie 1973: 28).

Eadie's research led him to consider whether there is in fact a
'helping personality'. In a subsequent article, based partly on the
above empirical research, and partly on an extensive study of the
literature, he concludes that among all the helping professions,
particularly among those who work within institutional structures,
there are certain common personality characteristics (Eadie 1975).

Working with Karen Horney's typology and description of neurotic trends, Eadie describes various aspects of 'the helping personality' in relation to ministers. Holding the idealized self-image of a loving person, the minister often finds it difficult to love himself. Further, this self-image may also lead him to the denial of any aggressive impulses. The clergy also find it difficult to live with failure to achieve objectives, blaming themselves even in circumstances beyond their control. Ministers also tend to be perfectionists who need to 'prove themselves' in perpetual activity and by constant availability. Called to be affectionate, loving and concerned, it is unacceptable to be blatantly sexual, erotic and carnal. Anger, hostility and even competitive self-assertion are equally unacceptable. Anxiety is relieved by conforming, by attempting to please others. Yet passive compliance can lead to resentment at manipulation by others, which in turn can lead to low-level depression and/or the somatization of stress. Eadie concludes by highlighting the need to inculcate greater self-awareness during training and by noting the reluctance of clergy to make use of therapeutic resources, a point to which I shall return.

In considering the incidence of stress among ministers it is possible both to exaggerate the extent of stress generally, and to underestimate the damage it causes in particular cases. Not all ministers feel themselves to be on the verge of burnout, and many even enjoy working under a degree of pressure. One consultation for ministers in mid-ministry indicated that, without exception, they were enjoying the challenges of this stage of their careers. It is of course possible that they were not being entirely honest, but there is no reason to believe this to be the case. While it must be recognized (as one of them pointed out) that they were the survivors, this group of ministers seemed happy and fulfilled and believed they were doing a worthwhile job in their parishes. Yet there are others who do not survive, and others who stagger on, and this latter group do not often attend consultations on ministry. However, attempts are being made to provide support and counselling for those in ministry.

The response of the Churches

Ministers are human. They experience stress – and distress – in their work and in their personal relationships in the same way as other people. Yet, paradoxically, those whose lives are dedicated to providing support and counsel for others often find it difficult to get help for themselves when they need it. There are a number of reasons for this state of affairs.

There is sometimes an unspoken assumption, for instance, on the part of congregations and even of ministers themselves, that the clergy should not experience problems of a personal nature. There can be a particular sense of betrayal in a congregation at the break-up of a clergy marriage or when some ministerial misdemeanour is reported in the press, especially when it is of a sexual nature. While there can be much loving care and support from congregations, there can also be a profound sense of disappointment, because in many ways the clergy carry people's unconscious projections of how things ought to be, and 'if ministers are not immune to personal breakdown then what hope is there for the rest of us?' For this reason, many clergy ignore the danger signals of stress until the symptoms of their distress become too obvious to hide.

There is also the assumption that when trouble comes, ministers have, or ought to have, through their faith, a special resource for coping. It is of course true that in their spiritual life many have found a source of strength which they know has come from beyond themselves, enabling them to cope with great personal pressures. Yet there are occasions when it is not enough to 'take it to the Lord in prayer'. Sometimes it is through the counsel of others, including the secular psychotherapist with a respect for the religious dimension of human experience, that prayer is answered and divine help most readily made available.

Different denominations have sought to address the issue in their own ways. In the Church of England, since 1986, a biennial consultation has been held at Launde Abbey, Leicestershire, sponsored by Diocesan Advisers in Pastoral Care and Counselling. Jacobs (1993b) traces developments since that first consultation when particular attention was paid to support groups; appraisal and assessment; training; and the resistance to the offer of care by clergy and their families. Subsequent consultations have continued to address these issues as well as related ones such as the relationship between the Adviser and the Bishop and diocese, job descriptions and contracts, and the need for a Code of Practice for pastoral care and counselling.

The Church of Scotland has set up a number of consultations, drawing on the resources and experience of the Alban Institute in Washington, DC, a research organization with a concern for ministry and congregational life. As a result of this initiative, a network of Presbytery Advisers has been established with a particular remit to develop systems of pastoral care of all those engaged in full-time ministry. Within presbyteries there has been a diversity of approach: one presbytery has appointed one of its senior members to act as chaplain to its ministers; another has set up a scheme of mutual support in which each minister is invited to nominate a fellow minister with whom they agree to consult regularly; yet again a presbytery may operate through a small group, keeping watch for ministerial ill-health, making sure that new members have at least one person to whom they can turn for help, and that support systems are in place. It has to be noted, however, that it is one thing for resources to be made available by a Church and quite another for them to be used by the clergy. There is some evidence that ministers, for reasons outlined above, prefer to find help outside the ecclesiastical structures.

Much of the above activity comes within the very necessary sphere of preventative pastoral care, providing the kind of support that should enable minor problems to be dealt with before they become major ones. Sometimes, however, more intense help is needed, help that is only available outside the Church. This can be expensive. Reference has already been made (p. 19) to the Guntrip Trust established under the umbrella of the Edinburgh-based Scottish Institute of Human Relations to allow ministers to make use of the facilities of the Institute. Bursaries are provided to enable ministers from Scotland and the North of England to receive personal therapy or to participate in analytic groups. While there is a concern to help the casualties of ministry, the underlying emphasis is educational rather than medical. The aim is personal learning and more self-awareness leading in turn to a greater depth of ministry to others.

In the Roman Catholic context, I have already noted (p. 35) the impressive work of Heronbrook House near Birmingham. The uniqueness of this institution lies in its ability to integrate high standards of psychotherapy without compromising its religious integrity. Its avowed aim is the counselling of priests and members of religious orders in a residential setting. Intensive individual and group psychotherapy sit comfortably alongside a Scripture Sharing Group and a Spirituality Seminar. Recognizing that all the residents are on a faith journey, the Scripture Sharing Group provides 'an opportunity to touch the faith of other community members, to share the same challenges, and to become even more aware of the broad journey that all share'. The purpose of the Spirituality Seminar is to 'help residents to become more aware of the spiritual dimension of life and to feel more comfortable in discussing spiritual values and needs in a group'. The emphasis is therefore on psychological and spiritual integration and on the affirmation of residents in their journey towards wholeness.

It is unlikely that there can be effective counselling of the clergy without some understanding of, and sympathy for, their internal frame of reference. This is necessary not only to enable them to draw on those aspects of their faith which are life-affirming, but also to facilitate the exploration of aspects of a religion which are patently life-constricting. The paradox is that while many ministers are happy to preach a gospel of grace, their pastoral practice demonstrates that their working theology is one of justification by works. Sometimes what ministers need to experience in the counselling relationship is the acceptance to which they point others but which they find so hard to claim for themselves.

In *Conflicts of the Clergy* (1964), one of the first books to address the issue of therapy with ministers, Margaret Bowers, an American psychotherapist, presents a profile of the successful therapist in the religious area:

> In the light of my experience I will advance four tentative propositions: (1) the therapist has undergone analysis of his own religious attitudes; (2) the therapist has had thorough training in the technique of the psychotherapy of religious conflicts; (3) the therapist has had orientation in the theology of the denomination of his patient, which means that the well-rounded therapist must acquaint himself with the theology of the Roman Catholic, the Jew and the Protestant; (4) *he must regard the patient's religious conflict as a core problem and respect the patient as a religious person.* If we accept the premise that successful therapy of religious personnel consists in reconciling the patient's *unconscious religious attitudes* with his *conscious theological attitude*, achieving a state where *theological truth and psychological truth coincide* – and I believe we must – then the successful therapist must definitely possess these four requirements.
>
> (Bowers 1964: 74)

The fulfilment of all Dr Bowers' requirements for those who counsel the clergy may be a counsel of perfection, particularly as regards a full understanding of the nuances of the theological differences among the denominations. What is certain is that effective therapy in this area demands a degree of religious self-understanding on the part of the therapist, and a respect for, if not agreement with, the theological position of the client. While these may be necessary conditions, they are not in themselves sufficient. What is also needed are therapists who are professionally competent, able to see religious defences for what they are. Yet the potential is there, through the counselling relationship itself, for therapists to enable ministers to move beyond religion to a faith that enriches their own lives, so that they, in turn, through their pastoral ministry, may enrich the lives of others.

RELATIONSHIPS WITH CONGREGATIONS

A distinctive feature of counselling in the pastoral and spiritual context is that normally it takes place in the context of a community of faith. Most of the clergy involved in a ministry of pastoral care do so within the context of a local congregation. Can insights derived from counselling enhance the life of the Church? Two areas are worthy of note. The first is in the development of lay pastoral care; the second in greater understanding of the dynamics of congregational life.

Lay pastoral care

I have already drawn attention to Lambourne's vision of pastoral care as 'lay, corporate, adventurous, variegated and diffuse' (Lambourne 1971:26). There is an increasing emphasis upon lay pastoral care within the Church. The question is whether this can ever be more than a pious hope of random and uncertain implementation, or whether it can be developed with intentionality and integrity.

One of the most thorough approaches to lay pastoral care is to be found in the work of Ronald Sunderland which he developed while on the staff of the Institute of Religion at the Texas Medical Center at Houston. An Australian Methodist minister, he trained as a CPE supervisor in Houston. In 1973 he was asked by a local minister to train a group of his elders for their pastoral ministry within the congregation. Theologically committed to the concept of lay ministry, Sunderland recognized that lay people, like ordinands, could not be trained through formal lectures. The methodological breakthrough came when participants in the course brought for review reports of pastoral visits they had made to members of the congregation during the previous week. What became apparent was the quality of the pastoral care already being offered by lay people, a quality that further training could only enhance. In this approach, lay people write up verbatim accounts of pastoral visits and are then normally supervised in groups, with individual supervision where necessary. Describing the main features of his training programme, Sunderland (1988) highlights: (a) the reading and reviewing of records of pastoral visits made by the lay people; (b) the use of the concept of 'story-listening', noting that most lay pastoral care consists of listening to stories of hardship, anxiety, grief, hurt or of celebration or achievement; (c) the discovery that story-listening can be applied to a wide range of pastoral situations such as hospitalization and bereavement and ministry to the housebound; (d) the fact that attention must be paid to the personal needs, emotions and limits of lay ministers, which will, if unrecognized, otherwise possibly intrude on their pastoral relationships; and (e) a recognition that lay pastoral care is integral to the wider ministry of the congregation.

It is obvious that this approach to lay ministry is essentially an application of the Clinical Pastoral Education model. It is equally obvious that if adopted, a new role emerges for ministers of congregations. Instead of being the sole providers of pastoral services they are involved in developing the skills of enabling others to become the providers. In effect ministers must learn the skills of supervision. There are factors that conspire against this. There is the expectation, held equally by ministers and congregations, that a visit by someone other than 'the minister' is somehow a second-class visit. Yet it is a model grounded theologically in the ministry of the whole religious community. And it is a model that can help to alleviate the impossible burdens carried by many parish clergy. The question is often whether the clergy are sufficiently secure in their own ministry to allow lay people to exercise their own pastoral skills, and whether they see it as their task 'to equip God's people for work in his service' (Ephesians, 4: 12, NEB).

The offer of pastoral care by others, not just by those ordained, is neither a new phenomenon nor a transatlantic one. A distinctive feature of the presbyterianism of my own Church of Scotland has been the office of the eldership which traditionally has shared with the minister the pastoral care of the congregation and parish. Each elder normally has pastoral care of a district consisting of fifteen to twenty families and routinely visits each three or four times a year. Good elders are also supportive at times of personal crisis. It must be recognized that among the ranks of the best elders are the women who have been ordained to this office within the past twenty-five years. In recent years the Church has been more systematic in the training of elders. A number of elder trainers, mostly lay and all voluntary, have been selected and trained nationally to work at the local level in presbyteries and congregations. Various courses are offered including a five-session module on Pastoral Care which includes training in basic listening skills and bereavement visiting.

While I have the most immediate knowledge of what is going on in my own church, I am also aware of increased emphasis on the ministry of the laity in other denominations and of new approaches to training. Some East Midland dioceses of the Church of England have produced a course for lay pastoral visitors in association with the University of Leicester's Centre for Pastoral Care and Counselling. Entitled 'I didn't seem to say very much . . .', this course is supported by two handbooks written for tutors and students (Cumming: 1989).

Another example is post-funeral follow-up of the bereaved, potentially one of the most valuable contributions of the Church to the mental health of individuals and communities. Normally, simply because of lack of time, it is impossible to do all that might be done. The Pastoral Foundation in Edinburgh has begun to train Bereavement Care teams from local congregations. Each team normally consists of the minister and four lay people who attend a course consisting of ten weekly meetings. They are introduced to the dynamics of grief and enabled to explore their own past experiences of loss. Some lay people who participate frequently bring to the task a wide experience of working with bereaved people in their professional lives (for example, recently retired nurses); others are simply gifted pastors with a natural bent for caring for others. Here, as in full-time ministry, selection and on-going supervision are vital; and again the full involvement of the minister is essential not only to provide information, and to suggest those who might be visited and to pave the way for the visits, but as a source of pastoral support for the team.

As always in congregations where lay pastoral care is developed, a different role and self-perception as well as new skills are required on the part of the ministers. Secure in their own ministry, unthreatened by the pastoral gifts of the laity, they themselves must possess certain counselling skills. They must be able to work effectively with lay people, knowing when to stay personally involved with the bereaved and when to make use of the team. It is important that such ministers know what resources for consultation are available for themselves and how to draw upon them. Despite its enormous potential, lay pastoral care makes demands on ministers and also introduces complexities into the life of a congregation. In order for that potential to be fully realized, ministers need, from time to time, to reflect upon their own management of the process.

Understanding congregations

Congregations are complex organizations and various tools have been devised to help us understand them better. *Building Effective*

Ministry (Dudley 1983) is a collection of essays analysing, from different perspectives, the life of a congregation in Wiltshire, a historic Massachusetts town. The congregation is considered from the point of view of psychology, ethnographic analysis, literary symbolism, sociology, theological ethics, philosophical theology and organizational development! The psychological analysis is by Barry Evans and Bruce Reed of the London-based Grubb Institute of Behavioural Studies. Drawing upon Bion's theory of groups (1961) they analyse the life of the Wiltshire congregation in terms of 'The Success and Failure of a Religious Club'. The congregation was 'a company church in a company town' initially dependent on the Adams family, the mill owners, for the provision of religion as for the basics of life. The authors demonstrate how, with the decline of the mill, dependence was transferred to one particular pastor who revived the congregation:

> It was reconstituted to meet the needs of a particular section of the population that symbolized and represented the town's Shangri-La mentality. This time the emotional needs were not so much for dependence upon some munificent provider but for expectancy, some hope for the future. In place of the dependent relationship between the congregation and the Adams family, there was a pairing relationship between the new pastor and the new members of the congregation. This expectancy found additional focus in the attention paid to children as the symbolic hope for the future. Because the expectancy was founded upon a fantasy (the idea of 'hope' never to be realized) it was bound to fail.
>
> We can now define the *primary task* of Wiltshire Church, which seems to characterize it from its foundation to the present. *To meet the emotional needs of its current congregation insofar as these reflect the dominant needs of the town of Wiltshire.*
>
> (Dudley 1983: 50)

To analyse the dynamics of a congregation in terms of the dependency needs being met undoubtedly gives us perspective on its life. The value of *Building Effective Ministry* is that different approaches can be considered together without falling into the trap of reductionism, psychological or otherwise. Indeed, it is impossible for a congregation to function simply on the basis of perceived needs. In an attempt to integrate the various approaches, Browning (1983) points out that some criteria are necessary to distinguish between authentic needs (for example, basic biological needs for food and clothing and needs for affiliation and mutual recognition) and needs which are culturally conditioned or distorted (for example, the need for the congregation to grow and be successful). Such criteria, which are ultimately ethical in nature, are also needed to help decide which authentic needs are to have the highest priority.

While Evans and Reed base their analysis of congregational life on the theory of group dynamics, James Dittes draws on a concept of central importance in psychotherapy itself. In *The Church in the Way* (1967) and *When the People Say No* (1979) Dittes finds parallels between the resistance encountered in psychotherapy and the resistance often met in the life of congregations. In psychotherapy, Dittes sees resistance not as a way used by clients to avoid looking at their problems but as an expression of these problems:

> If a patient could ideally adopt the role of patient, effectively, maturely and adaptably without getting in his own way, without frustrating his and others' objectives, he wouldn't need to be a patient. If the patient could face, without flinching or defence, the feelings and facts of his life which provoke resistance in therapy, then he could handle these outside of therapy and wouldn't be there.
>
> (Dittes 1967: 50)

Resistance in psychotherapy must be understood because the understanding of the resistance may itself be the key to understanding the underlying problem.

Resistance (especially to change) is also common in congregational life. I have pointed out that more and more lay people find themselves in a ministry of pastoral care. Yet there are many congregations where nothing very much seems to happen and everything is left to 'the minister'. This can happen even in congregations where there are many lay people used to taking responsibility in their secular jobs. But at church meetings, something seems to happen to them. Proposals for greater lay involvement in pastoral ministry are resisted with a disproportionate amount of energy. It is as though, in a church setting, intelligent people become part of a dependency culture.

Resistance can be understood in terms of some of the defence mechanisms that give expression to the resistance which may be integral to any counselling relationship. The statement that 'People only want a visit from the minister' may be an example of *projection* uttered by those who themselves do not want to be visited by lay people; those who vote for a new programme with enthusiasm but 'regretfully' find themselves too busy to participate personally may be displaying a form of *reaction formation*; and those who are seeking in the church to be cared for rather than to be involved in reaching out to others can readily be seen to experience *regression*.

In his understanding of resistance in congregational life, Dittes saw similar positive aspects as in the process of psychotherapy. Resistance is not necessarily a sign of personal opposition to the minister, nor of pure cussedness on the part of those who fail to co-operate in agreed plans.

The understanding of resistance may give a clue to what stirs people most deeply. People offer resistance at the point where they feel most deeply. An authoritarian attack on resistance is, therefore, invariably counterproductive. It is important to understand the underlying fears and motives and to discover the meaning of the resistance. Dittes is offering a psychologically sophisticated understanding of ministry, one in which the pastor's self-understanding and an understanding of the dynamics of individuals and groups can enable creativity to grow from a sensitive handling of the difficulties inherent in the life of any congregation. It is at this point that skill and experience in counselling can facilitate an understanding of people in congregations.

RELATIONSHIPS WITH PARENT CHURCHES

The relationship between pastoral counsellors and their parent churches has not been uniformly positive. This has been true, at least to some extent, for many in the specialized ministries of the churches. When the news became public that I was leaving parish ministry for hospital chaplaincy, more than one fellow minister added to somewhat muted congratulations 'I am so sorry you are leaving "the ministry".' It was as though the parish ministry was not only the normative ministry of the church, but the only one worthy of being considered as a ministry. Nor has it always been easy for clergy who have left parish work to become full-time counsellors to continue to exercise some kind of ministry within the Church. I know of at least one counsellor who was refused a bishop's licence permitting him to officiate within the diocese. 'You cannot have your cake and eat it' was the somewhat insensitive episcopal response to a man who wanted to affirm his priesthood as well as his vocation as a counsellor.

If it is sometimes difficult for clergy-counsellors to find a niche within the Church, there are also factors, within the structures of the Church itself, which can make it difficult for ministers to find skilled pastoral help. Whether authority is embodied in individuals such as bishops or provincial moderators, or in church courts or committees, it is not easy to separate the structures of authority from the structures of pastoral care. This does not mean that those within the churches who have a concern for the pastoral support of ministers have not been aware of this problem and tried to circumvent it. That is not the point. The point is that a minister in distress may imagine that to seek help within the Church may be personally damaging, that 'they' will know he has a problem, that 'everyone' will get to know about it, and that his future career prospects will be permanently damaged. In these fantasies, there may or may not be elements of truth.

As I have already indicated, there is now a recognition that those who work full-time in the service of the Church sometimes need help. Hopefully a culture is emerging when it is recognized that to seek help when it is necessary is not a confession of weakness but a manifestation of strength and integrity, and that the best pastors are those wounded healers who have experienced both pain and renewal. To take the risk of seeking help may be an act of personal courage and also the beginning of personal and professional renewal. There are occasions when it is better that the help should be given by someone who understands the external circumstances and the internal frame of reference of the client. In this respect counsellors who have themselves served in parish settings or in other ministries are peculiarly well-placed to offer help and support. What is important is that counsellors who have left church appointments for other spheres of service should be sufficiently in touch with their own reasons for making the change. Counsellors who have failed to resolve their own love-hate relationship with Mother Church are not likely to be the right people to help struggling parish clergy take the right decisions about their future ministry!

I began this chapter by pointing to the place of pastoral counsellors within a much wider network of care and support. I have tried to demonstrate the complexity of the counsellor's role within that network. The pastoral counsellor is no *deus ex machina* who descends from on high to dispense expertise. An integral part of the community, those who function as pastoral counsellors need to be aware of the complexity of the context and of their roles within it. What cannot be changed needs to be understood and managed. It is in their awareness of the complexity of professional relationships that those who counsel in the pastoral and spiritual context may make one of their most significant contributions to the health of communities and individuals.

· SIX ·

A critique of counselling in the pastoral and spiritual context

When, in 1927, Freud wrote *The Future of an Illusion*, the illusion he referred to was religion – and it had no future (Shaw 1978: 17). Nearly seventy years on, religion survives as a potent phenomenon in contemporary culture. Freud would perhaps have been surprised by the fact that religion is frequently inextricably bound up with psychotherapeutic endeavours that are rooted in his concepts and professional practice. Yet some religious people have found realities in his work, and in the work of other therapists who have built on his ideas, which have transformed their understanding of those caring relationships that belong within communities of faith.

Even in the 1960s, the future of the religious illusion looked decidedly problematic. This was the decade of secularization and a further marginalization of the institutional church. If religion was to survive, the Gospel would require, so it was argued, a secular meaning for secular cities in which God was dead. This secular decade also saw the proliferation of the humanistic therapies and the offer of salvation through self-realization. It has been suggested, with some reason, that these humanistic therapies sometimes felt like new expressions of an optimistic faith.

The quest for meaning continues unabated and the continued existence of religious belief and practice surely says something about its durability in this search. The preceding chapters have pointed to various ways in which religion, far from being supplanted by humanism and its therapies, has indeed taken these therapies into itself and, as the churches have done throughout history, incorporated them in the service of traditional ministries of pastoral care.

Yet religion has not simply been content to accommodate itself to the spirit of the age. A surprising feature of the late twentieth century has been a revival of interest in a wide range of spiritualities, what Michael Northcott calls a 'resurgence of the sacred' (1992). Far from accommodating itself to the *zeitgeist*, a recrudescent religion has, on occasion, expressed itself in conservative and even fundamentalist forms. This applies not only to Christianity but to other world religions in which radical elements have sought political as well as a spiritual influence.

Thus the contemporary context of every form of counselling is characterized by a religious pluralism. The mainstream Christian denominations, with some congregations exhibiting signs of excitement and vitality amidst apparent institutional decline, continue to function alongside charismatic and independent churches for whom church growth is a reality. Other world religions are acquiring a foothold within Western culture as evidenced, for example, by Buddhist monks establishing a retreat centre on Holy Isle off the west coast of Scotland. The fascination for many people of New Age manifestations of spirituality has already been alluded to. Postmodernism is surely right in its thesis that there now exist few, if any, of the shared stories, beliefs and values that gave social cohesion to previous generations.

It is perhaps not entirely accidental that the emergence of a more pluralistic society and the disappearance of these commonly held stories, beliefs and values has been accompanied by the growth of the counselling movement. In an age when shared stories seem to be losing their potency, it becomes more important than ever that people should make sense of their own personal stories. I have tried to show in the previous chapters that counselling in the pastoral and spiritual context has a special concern to help people find meaning in these personal stories. It is not for counsellors to *impose* a meaning that has its roots in their own personal stories. That said, it cannot be imagined that counsellors will be able to distance themselves from their own background, for 'the pastoral counselor is not only a listener to stories; he or she is also a bearer of stories and of a story' (Gerkin 1984: 27). It is important that counsellors should be aware of all the different stories that are present in any counselling situation. These will include the client or parishioner's own life-story, the counsellor's story, and stories and myths that may be part of a shared culture or community of faith. One of the tasks in the training and supervision of carers and counsellors is to enable them to understand the place of these stories both in the lives of their clients and in the counselling process itself, a task which has been explored in detail elsewhere (Foskett and Lyall 1988). Here I examine some of the contemporary issues related to training in pastoral care and counselling.

TRAINING

Those who find themselves counselling in the pastoral and spritual context come to it by a variety of routes. I have already drawn attention to the way in which the routine pastoral work of the clergy can develop into a counselling ministry of some depth. How far do present methods of theological education equip clergy for this task? I have also noted the fact that the majority of people attending training courses in this context are lay women. What is the nature of the training offered to them?

Theological education and pastoral counselling

In the universities and theological colleges where women and men are trained for full-time ministry, it is undeniable that Pastoral Studies is given a much higher profile today than a generation ago. A recent study of theological training in Britain (Bunting 1990) sets out the current situation. A high priority is given to classroom teaching in the area of Pastoral Studies, together with supervised field education in local church settings and secular agencies. In the local church, the role of the incumbent as supervisor is crucial; and there are indications that theological colleges are now taking seriously the training in supervisory skills of those with 'hands-on' responsibility for the field education of ordinands. Hopefully this will produce cohorts of clergy with a degree of self-awareness and competence as pastoral carers. But does the system produce ministers who are skilled as pastoral *counsellors*? As a university teacher in the discipline of Pastoral Studies, I have to say that it does not and cannot.

There are factors inherent in theological education which, at present, militate against producing skilled counsellors. The first is time. The study of pastoral care may only be part of the single *required* course designed to cover the work of the ordained ministry. In one brief module, educational priorities must be limited and clearly defined. Developing a preliminary understanding of the pastoral task, knowing something of the relevance of human growth and development for that task, realizing the need for active listening as opposed to the giving of advice, gaining some understanding of the dynamics of loss, and becoming aware of the pervasiveness of transference and counter-transference in pastoral relationships may seem a heavy (possibly too heavy) agenda for an introductory module. If, however, it is the only required course, it is necessary to provide a 'map of the territory' so that ordinands have some idea of what is involved in pastoral ministry. More advanced optional courses may be made available which combine further academic input with more experiential modes of teaching and learning, together with relevant supervised placement work. I have an impression, however, that those who take advanced elective courses in pastoral care and counselling are those who already possess a natural gift for pastoral work, and that others who would benefit from them find it hard to take the risk of exposing themselves to more experiential modes of learning.

This points to a second difficulty in providing training in counselling within the context of theological education. Not everyone who is selected as a candidate for the ministry has either the inclination or the aptitude to train as a counsellor. This is not necessarily a fact to be deplored because the Church needs its preachers and teachers and social activists, as well as its pastors and counsellors. The qualities required for success in one role may not be those needed in another. There is, however, a matter to be considered in relation to *all* these different ministries: the capacity of ordinands for self-awareness. Nicholas Bradbury, Director of Pastoral Studies at an Anglican theological college, has identified this as a real problem in pastoral education: 'not so much that of aptitude as of attitude' (Bradbury 1992: 10). In the culture of psychotherapy, it is taken for granted that trainees will be enabled to get in touch with those needs of their own which have brought them into training. In preparation for ministry, however, these needs tend to be denied or wrapped up in piety. Bradbury's concern was that 'it had not yet dawned on candidates that *in order to train as pastors they would be training to use their selves as a tool for their work'*. Bradbury describes how his field-education programme was reshaped along more psychodynamic principles with regular opportunities for students to explore their own inner world and the ministries in which they were involved. It may well be that Bradbury's article, while lamenting the present situation, is itself a sign of hope.

The training of pastoral counsellors

No matter how much emphasis a college or university department gives to pastoral counselling, it cannot turn out ordinands who are also accredited pastoral counsellors. Within the normal Bachelor of Divinity degree or its equivalent there is simply no room for that degree of specialization. I have always encouraged students with a special interest in counselling to seek a 'proper' training in one of the many counselling training courses now available. There is much to be said for ministers training in secular settings. It is not more theological insights that they need at such a point, but a thorough grounding in counselling theory and practice, with the kind of supervision that challenges their presuppositions. Unless they are determined to live in two worlds, good supervision also helps them to integrate new theoretical insights and practical skills with their personal theologies, both explicit and implicit. They begin to make what David Tracy calls 'mutually critical correlations' between theology and practice (Tracy 1983: 65). The encounter with human suffering causes new questions to be addressed to their academic theologies; their own appropriation of the Christian story becomes ` part of their pastoral understanding; theology becomes alive and relevant; practice is deepened.

The Westminster Pastoral Foundation's network of associated and affiliated counselling centres, with its requirement that certain minimum standards be attained, has been an invaluable national resource for training. Tyndall's comments on training in a companion volume *Counselling in the Voluntary Sector* (1993) are also relevant in this context, because generally church-related centres are almost inevitably part of the voluntary sector. Such training normally involves the provision of a knowledge base, an opportunity for experiential learning and self-discovery and supervised practice in counselling. Despite WPF's past agonizing over its understanding of what it means to be a *Pastoral* Foundation (see Chapter Four), questions of meaning and value are still central to its training programme. Looking back on twenty-one years of WPF, Mary Ann Coate, their Director of Training, writes:

> we are probably the only training organization to mount a core seminar on *ontology* and to address the great 'Why' questions as well as those I call the 'What' and the 'How' questions. *Why* do any of us do this sort of work? What values do we bring to it and what is the meaning of it for us, individually and corporately? I think that what has taken place is a shift from the centrality of the answers to the centrality of the questions.
>
> (Coate 1991: 16)

A different system of training may be seen in the Diploma in Pastoral Counselling offered by the Extension Studies Department of St John's Theological College, Nottingham. Validated by Nottingham University, this is a distance-learning course that seeks to integrate a Christian perspective with a rigorous study of both human growth and development and different methods of counselling. Intensive personal work in a local group and the supervised practice of counselling are effectively combined with a system of distance tutors, local supervision and occasional visits to the College.

For anyone who wishes to train as a counsellor in this context there are a number of options. All of them involve a high degree of commitment in terms of money and time, together with a degree of personal discomfort. The best of the courses do not allow students to qualify without a deep encounter with themselves in relation to both motives and values. But they produce women and men who make a real contribution to healing the hurts of individuals and communities. That in so doing the counsellors gain much satisfaction will surprise no one, least of all the counsellors themselves, because training inevitably makes us aware of the strange mixture of motives that lead us into a ministry of pastoral care and counselling.

ACCREDITATION AND CERTIFICATION

Closely related to the issue of training are those of accreditation and certification. The distinction between these terms is a fine one but, at least in the American literature, the former has been used mainly with reference to validating the standards of training institutions and courses, while the latter has referred to the attestation of the professional competence of individuals.

It is only with the recent rapid developments in counselling that this has become a matter of some importance. When pastoral care was viewed solely as a function of the clergy, ordination to the ministry was seen a sufficient licence to exercise their ministry of pastoral care using such methods as that felt to be within their competence. This has been the dominant view throughout the history of the Church's ministry and one from which few would wholly dissent today. The issue, however, is far from simple, as illustrated by the following legal case which provoked widespread interest in the United States.

In 1979, a twenty-four-year old man called Kenneth Nally shot himself, having at various times received counselling from four of the pastors of Grace Community Church in the San Fernando Valley in California. His parents sued the church because, so they believed, the church had 'filled their son with guilt, guilt, guilt'. It was ten years later before the US Supreme Court refused to hear the case. What is significant about it is the degree of support that Grace Community Church received right across the spectrum of the Christian churches. Grace Community Church was a large, independent, fundamentalist congregation running its own Christian counselling centre and training programme. Their theoretical base, theological presuppositions and counselling practice would certainly not have received universal approval within the pastoral counselling movement, but there was a substantial issue uniting all the churches:

> Virtually every major religious group in the United States contributed to Grace Church's defense, including both mainline and fundamentalist denominations. Even the Catholic church, which Grace Church head pastor McArthur was alleged to have described as 'evil' joined in supporting Grace Church's defense . . . as did the National Council of Churches and the American Association of Pastoral Counselors. Virtually all of those feared that if the case were decided – regardless of whether the decision were in favor of the plaintiffs or the defendants – it would stifle religious counselling by (in the words of the trial court judge) 'opening the floodgates to clergy malpractice litigation'.
> (Battin 1990: 210)

Although the American Association of Pastoral Counselors joined in the defence of the right of congregation to engage in pastoral ministry free from the fear of malpractice litigation, that organization has also been in the forefront of the setting of professional standards for pastoral care and counselling. Together with the Association for Clinical Pastoral Education, AAPC has been instrumental in establishing procedures for the accreditation of training centres and the certification of practitioners, especially those of the latter group who sell their services on the open market as it were. A particular emphasis in ACPE has been the accreditation of its supervisors at various levels ensuring a consistent quality in the training of those students, ministers and lay people who enrol in its large number of programmes (over three hundred) throughout North America.

In Britain, moves towards accreditation and certification have been somewhat halting. As I indicated in Chapter One, when it was proposed to establish a national pastoral organization in 1971, it was anticipated that one of its tasks would be to set common standards for training and practice. I then drew attention to the formative influence at that time of the late Bob Lambourne and of his protest against the setting-up of a British counselling organization which would be 'accredited, hierarchical . . . professional . . . standardized, defined' (see p. 28). Lambourne undoubtedly did much to declericalize and demedicalize pastoral counselling in Britain. It is also probably true that, wittingly or unwittingly, he set back the process of accreditation and the setting of professional standards in the pastoral field. In fact, the accreditation vacuum was filled by at least two of the major pastoral organizations for themselves. In 1977 the Westminster Pastoral Foundation established its own Institute of Pastoral Education and Counselling (IPEC), giving its own graduates a professional home. In 1988, under pressure to assert its psycho-therapeutic identity, IPEC became the Institute of Psychotherapy and Counselling (WPF), in which the Pastoral retained a latent pre-sence in WPF. For a number of years the Clinical Theology Asso-ciation has had a careful system for the authorization and evaluation of its own tutors and assistant tutors. There is also a Minimum Code of Practice which includes adherence to the Association's *Statement of Ethics* and an understanding that tutors will be in some kind of personal supervision.

It is of course open to pastoral counsellors to seek accreditation through the British Association for Counselling and many do so. The Association for Pastoral Care and Counselling, one of the divi-sions of BAC, has recently explored the broader issues relating to the need for the recognition and accreditation of pastoral work. Two thousand questionnaires were distributed to the readers of *Contact* and to others involved in pastoral work. Preliminary findings were reported in a subsequent issue of the journal (Foskett 1993: 21): one hundred and sixty six people replied, identifying themselves almost equally as either pastoral carers or pastoral coun-sellors; one hundred and thirteen were involved in parish and com-munity work, fifty-three in pastoral studies and and sixty-three in various kinds of chaplaincies (some placed themselves in more than one category). Sixty-nine per cent were in favour of a scheme of accreditation which they believed would provide for the consist-ency that people had a right to expect from pastors; it would dis-tinguish levels of skill and expertise and enhance professionalism among pastoral workers. Others emphasized the importance of networking and of providing a basis for referral. A significant minority were against any national scheme of recognition. Some felt that pastoral work was too broad either to define or to evaluate; others felt that good pastors would be excluded and their work devalued by a recognition scheme. One correspondent argued that the best accreditation scheme was already in place – 'they either come back or they don't!'; the most passionate opponents of ac-creditation claimed it is élitist, exclusive and pedantic.

What is clear is that within those engaged in pastoral care and counselling, there is certainly no consensus about the need for ac-creditation. In this respect there seems to be a significant difference from those engaged in counselling in other contexts where some kind of accreditation or certification is necessary before counselling can be offered, whether in the voluntary sector or private practice. In such cases, accreditation is often a goal to be achieved and a status to be prized. It may well be that the readership of *Contact* provides a skewed population for this kind of survey. As a former editor of the journal, I suspect that a preponderance of its readership is drawn from the ranks of the ordained clergy. If so, it may well be that those ordained see no need for further accreditation, believing their ordination to be sufficient authorization for their ministry. This, however, does nothing to address the needs of the hundreds of people who counsel in this context but are not ordained; nor does it provide a means of ensuring the competence of or strengthening the confidence of those clergy who wish to work with people in depth. What the report also demonstrates is that, at least among those who responded to the questionnaire, those opposed to any form of accreditation are in a minority. It may well be that other external pressures will become important factors in this discussion.

A development that has significant consequences for many different professions and activities, including counselling, is the advent of National Vocational Qualifications (NVQs). In 1988 the National Council for Vocational Qualifications (in Scotland, the Scottish Council for Vocational Qualifications) was established. Supported by the Confederation of British Industries, the Trade Unions Congress and the Government, this is an attempt to make vocational qualifications relevant to the work-place. This scheme in intended to operate industry-wide and not just for counsellors. In a private paper prepared for the Clinical Theology Association, Michael Weatherley (1993) writes:

> Traditionally people were qualified by demonstrating they had absorbed units of knowledge. Assessment for qualifications will shift to outputs, that is the ability to do the job . . . A unit of competence defines and measures a predefined standard of competent performance . . . No longer will largely irrelevant academic qualifications be the basis of defining the ability to do the job. Training will be expected to have taken place, particularly in the background theory. There will also be the need to demonstrate and record the ability to work at a consistent level based on the observation of actual performance . . . Various centres provide both the training necessary.

There is something to be said for this concept. People who are good at passing examinations – even in the theory of counselling –

do not necessarily make good counsellors. If this scheme produces competent counsellors, so much to the good. Yet questions must be asked – and hopefully answered. It may simply be my present academic context that leads me to detect an anti-intellectual bias in these proposals. Lip-service appears to be being paid to a prior conceptual framework; yet the overall impression is of a downgrading of a theoretical understanding of the counselling process. We should not forget the adage that there is nothing so practical as a good theory. More fundamentally, we must also guard against methods of assessment based on so-called performance criteria that miss the deeper nuances of human interaction. And if this is true of counselling in general, how much more of counselling in the pastoral and spiritual context, which may encompass yet another of the complex dimensions of the human spirit?

THE WAY AHEAD

I began this book with an assertion that counselling in a pastoral and spiritual context is characterized by complexity. My aim in the previous chapters has been to shed some light on the multifarious relationships of counselling in this context to contemporary culture with its strange mixture of religion and secularism. It is unlikely that the future will be any less complex. There are certain perils in the pathway of anyone who tries assume the mantle of prophet. First, it is difficult enough to discern current trends in any discipline, without trying to predict what will happen next. A personal perspective is no more than that, and even a personal perspective based on evidence necessarily depends upon what is seen from one particular viewpoint. Second, it is hard to distinguish what we *think* will happen from what we believe *ought* to happen. With these provisos, I believe it is possible to identify certain trends in counselling within the pastoral and spiritual context and to look a little further down the road to see where they might be leading us.

1   In the context of training for the ordained ministry of the Christian church, the last generation has undoubtedly seen much more training in this area. Hopefully this will continue to develop with a greater awareness of both its strengths and limitations. A danger of increased emphasis on the professional training of counsellors is a devaluation of the Church's traditional ministry of pastoral care. There is a need to reaffirm the integrity of pastoral care as a part of the life of the Church which brings support, encouragement and comfort to many within local congregations and in the wider

community. Yet part of the integrity of pastoral care is a recognition of its limitations. While those engaged in pastoral care will make good use of certain counselling skills, those carers also need to recognize the boundaries of their competence and to be aware that they are not therapists and to develop skills in referral. There is only one person more dangerous that an untrained counsellor and that is a partly trained counsellor who thinks they are adequately trained.

2   Again within the context of the Christian church, there is now much greater emphasis on the pastoral task of local congregations. This is to be welcomed because this is where pastoral care belongs. In an important, but seldom quoted paper, E. Mansell Pattison, an American psychiatrist, introduces the concept of 'Systems Pastoral Care' drawing out for pastoral care the implications of developments in social and community psychiatry. Drawing upon general systems theory, Pattison sees a more than positive role for local congregations in the prevention and detection of human distress and in rehabilitation should breakdown occur:

> Were pastoral care to be designed on the model of preventive medicine it would become *systems pastoral care*. Leaders would be trained to deal with social systems at many levels and to function as enablers – enabling the church to become a center of moral enquiry, a center of personal learning and growth, for human sustenance and nourishment and for human reparation. The pastor would not do all this himself but would craft a social system that functions preventively at many levels.
>
> (Pattison 1972: 2)

It might be argued that to draw on the concepts of social psychiatry is simply to move from one medical model to another, from one based on the cure of disease to another based on its prevention. Yet it is not difficult to see such concepts as 'moral enquiry', 'personal learning', 'human sustenance' and 'reparation' as not far from the Kingdom of God and indeed rooted in the theology and concerns of the Christian church.

Integral to a renewed emphasis on the local congregation as the context of pastoral care has been the discovery (or rediscovery) of the pastoral gifts of many lay people. This new role for congregations, and for lay people within them, makes quite different demands on the ordained leadership of the Church. To be able to share the pastoral task, to enable and to trust others without seeking to control them, to be aware of congregational processes without needing to know all the details of what is going on, calls for different skills, different training, different attitudes, perhaps even a different theology of church and ministry. These issues need to be addressed not only in pastoral training but throughout the whole process of selection and training for ministry.

3   This emphasis on pastoral care in the congregation is not meant to detract in any way from the important contribution of many who in recent years have subjected themselves to intensive training in counselling and who have acquired specialized skills. They are a gift to churches and communities, the value of which is not sufficiently appreciated. I suspect that the church is somewhat ambivalent towards counselling and counsellors. It can be regarded as a kind of 'dumping ground' to which 'difficult people' are sent to be 'sorted out'. When it is realized that there are no 'quick fixes', or when those who seek or are referred for counselling become aware of the personal commitment required in terms of time and self-revelation (and sometimes of money), there can be a sense of disappointment. There can also be a reluctance to use the services counsellors offer, either personally or in referring others. In Chapter Five I drew attention to some of the anxieties that religious people experience in relation to counselling, especially with regard to the possibility that counselling might undermine faith. To these we might add the perception, and perhaps the reality, that those engaged in pastoral counselling are not normally the most conservative of people. An acceptance of people as they are, in their strength and in their vulnerability, which is integral to the process of counselling can often be mistaken for a moral relativism. Continuing deep encounters with their fellow human-beings and an awareness of the complexity of circumstance and behaviour which can lead to disfunction does not lead counsellors into hasty judgements about people. This can be quite disorienting to some religious people who live in a world where the only colours are black and white.

We need more counsellors who are both highly competent as counsellors or therapists and sensitive to the transcendent and spiritual dimensions of human existence. There are too many people around who set themselves up as counsellors of every kind with little or no training. Whatever form of accreditation emerges in years to come, there is little doubt that those who offer their services to the public as counsellors in *any* context must be required to reach acceptable standards of competence. In the pastoral and spiritual context we need competent counsellors able to enter the faith world of those whom they seek to help, and to help them draw on the resources of their faith. They must also, however, be able to detect the difference between an unhelpful religion and a nurturing faith, a difference explored in various ways by Fromm

(1950) when he contrasted humanitarian and authoritarian religions, and by Rokeach (1960) in his discussion of the open and closed mind.

4   Those who counsel in the pastoral and spiritual context will continue to do so straddling a number of boundaries. Like all counsellors they will work on the interface of theory and practice, allowing theoretical perspectives to illuminate their practice and their practice to pose fresh questions for their theories. As pastoral counsellors, they will also function on the boundary of religious belief and counselling, their attitudes and practice to others shaped by their willingness to listen with reverence to stories and faith journeys, their clients and their own, as well as the insights of other faiths. They will counsel in a context of complementary, if not competing, spiritualities, affirming within themselves the truths and the stories which have shaped them, yet appreciating the truths of the stories which are meaningful to others.

To talk of the truthfulness of stories raises an issue that some might consider to be of some theological significance. Is there a story which is universally true? I suspect that among my readers I will have at least two very different groups of critics. On the one hand, those who are not Christians, or whose attachment to any established religion is a best tenuous, may feel that I have identified myself too much with my own Christian tradition and neither listened to, nor understood, the stories of other individuals and traditions. On the other hand, many of my fellow Christians may accuse me of relativism with regard to the truth of the Gospel and the uniqueness of Jesus Christ in his power to heal and save. For them the only true story is the Christian story and the task of the pastoral counsellor is shaped by that unique truth. To those who feel I may have identified myself too much with my own tradition, I can only admit to being who I am, a minister of the Church of Scotland, shaped by my own story of faith and family and relationships and professional experiences. I hope that others will in turn write from their perspective of counselling in the pastoral and spiritual context that I and others may learn from them. To those of my fellow Christians who may feel that, in being open to the truth of other stories, I have compromised the truth of the Gospel, I would simply affirm my belief that the truths of the Christian faith are not essentially propositional, but rather are relational: that 'the Word became flesh and dwelt among us, full of grace and truth' (St John, I: 14. RSV). In my pastoral relationships I can only be who I am; similarly those to whom I have the privilege to minister, and those with whom I work, can only be who they are. Yet the miracle of grace is that in the complexity and the simplicity of the pastoral relationship, when we have offered the best of our understanding and our skills, the God of all grace is at work deep within the human spirit with a power that transcends and encompasses all our knowing and all our skill.

References

Adams, J. E. (1973) *The Christian Counselor's Manual*. Grand Rapids: Baker.

Ainsworth-Smith, I. and Speck, P. (1982) *Letting Go: Caring for the Dying and Bereaved*. London: SPCK.

Anderson, S. M. (1990) 'Psychology and Mythology', *Dictionary of Pastoral Care and Counselling*. Nashville: Abingdon.

Ashby, H. U. (1982) 'Kohut's Contribution to Pastoral Care', *Journal of Supervision and Training in Ministry*, Volume 5. Chicago: ACPE and AAPC.

Barth, K. (1961) *Church Dogmatics*, III, 4. Edinburgh: T. & T. Clark.

Battin, M. P. (1990) *Ethics in the Sanctuary*. New Haven: Yale.

Benner, D. G. (1988) *Psychotherapy and the Spiritual Quest*. London: Hodder & Stoughton.

Bion, W. R. (1961) *Experiences in Groups*. London: Tavistock.

Black, D. (1991) *A Place for Exploration: the Story of the Westminster Pastoral Foundation 1969–90*. London: WPF.

Bloomfield, I. (1991) 'The Dympna Centre: Memories and Reflections', *Contact*, 106.

Bonhoeffer, D. (1959) *The Cost of Discipleship*. London: SCM.

Bowers, M. (1964) *Conflicts of the Clergy*. New York: Nelson.

Bradbury, N. (1992) 'Is The Church of England Serious About Training Pastors?', *Contact*, 108.

Breech, J. (1989) *Jesus and Postmodernism*. Minneapolis: Augsburg.

British Association for Counselling (1992) *Code of Ethics and Practice for Counsellors*. BAC: Rugby.

British Council of Churches (1968) *Pastoral Care and the Training of Ministers*.

Browning, D. (1983) 'Integrating the Approaches', *Building Effective Ministry*, (ed.) Dudley. New York: Harper & Row.

Bryant, C. (1983) *Jung and the Christian Way*. London: Darton, Longman and Todd.

Bunting, I. D. (1990) *The Places to Train*. London: MARC Europe.

Burck, R. (1978) 'From the word to the conversation', *Pastoral Psychology*, 27, 2, 91–104.

Cabot, R. C. (1926) 'A Plea for a Clinical Year in the Course of Theological Education', *Adventures on the Borderland of Ethics*. New York: Harper and Bros.

Campbell, A. V. (1985) *Paid to Care?* London: SPCK.

Campbell, A. V. (1986) *Rediscovering Pastoral Care*, 2nd edn. London: Darton, Longman and Todd.

Campbell, A. V. (1990) 'Lambourne, Robert A.', *Dictionary of Pastoral Care and Counseling*. Nashville: Abingdon.

Capps, D. (1993) *The Depleted Self: Sin in a Narcissistic Age*. Minneapolis: Fortress.

Chaplin, J. (1993) 'Counselling and gender', *Handbook of Counselling in Britain* (ed.) Dryden *et al*. London: Routledge.

Church of Scotland (1993a) *Report to the General Assembly of the Board of Ministry*, 292–4.

Church of Scotland (1993b) *Report to the General Assembly of the Board of Social Responsibility*, 490–6.

Clebsch, W. A. and Jaekle, C. R. (1964) *Pastoral Care in Historical Perspective*. New York: Harper Torchbooks.

Clinebell, H. J. (1966) *Basic Types of Pastoral Counseling*. Nashville: Abingdon. (2nd edn published 1984 as *Basic Types of Pastoral Care and Counseling*)

Clinebell, H. J. (1971) 'Response to Lambourne', *Contact*, 36.

Coate, M. A. (1991) 'WPF Training 20 Years On', *Contact*, 106.

Congo, D. G. (1990) 'Burnout', *Dictionary of Pastoral Care and Counseling*. Nashville: Abingdon.

Cooper, H. (1988) *Soul Searching: Studies in Judaism and Psychotherapy*. London: SCM.

Crabb, L. J. (1975) *Basic Principles of Biblical Counseling*. Grand Rapids: Zondervan.

Crabb, L. J. (1977) *Effective Biblical Counseling*. Grand Rapids: Zondervan.

Cramond, W. A. (1970) 'Psychotherapy and the Dying Patient', *British Medical Journal*, 3, 389–93.

Crites, S. (1971) 'The Narrative Quality of Experience', *Journal of the American Academy of Religion*, 291–311.

Cumming, S. (1989) 'I didn't seem to say very much . . .'. University of Leicester Department of Adult Education.

Cupitt, D. (1986) *Life Lines*. London: SCM.

Dechant, P. (1991) 'Confidentiality and the Pastoral Minister: Duty, Right or Privilege?' *Journal of Pastoral Care*, XLV, 1.

Diocese of Bristol (1990) *Towards a Code of Practice for Pastoral Care by the Clergy*.

Dittes, J. E. (1961) 'Psychology and a Ministry of Faith', *The Ministry and Mental Health*. New York: Association Press.

Dittes, J. E. (1967) *The Church in the Way*. New York: Scribners.

Dittes, J. E. (1979) *When the People Say No*. San Francisco: Harpers.

Drakeford, J. W. (1990) 'Integrity Therapy', *Dictionary of Pastoral Care and Counseling*. Nashville: Abingdon.

Draper, E. *et al*. (1965) 'On the Diagnostic Value of Religious Ideation', *Archives of General Psychiatry*, 13.

Dudley, C. S. (ed.) (1983) *Building Effective Ministry*. New York: Harper & Row.

Eadie, H. A. (1972) 'Health of Scottish Clergymen'. *Contact*, 41.

Eadie, H. A. (1973) 'Psychological Health of Clergymen', *Contact*, 42.

Eadie, H. A. (1975) 'The Helping Personality', *Contact*, 49.

Education for Pastoral Ministry (1976). London: Church of England's Advisory Council for the Church's Ministry (ACCM).

Ekstein, R. and Wallerstein, R. S. (2nd edn 1972) *The Teaching and Learning of Psychotherapy*. New York: International Universities Press.

Eliot, T. S. (1950) *The Cocktail Party*. London: Faber & Faber.

Erikson. E. (1965) *Childhood and Society*. London: Penguin.

Evans, H. B. and Reed, B. (1983) 'The Success and Failure of a Religious Club' *Building Effective Ministry*, (ed.) Dudley. New York: Harper & Row.

Farrah, L. (1993) 'The Good Soul Guide', *The Scotsman*, 25 September.

Fitchett, G. (1993) *Spiritual Assessment in Pastoral Care: A Guide to Selected Resources*. Journal of Pastoral Care Monograph: Atlanta.

Fletcher, B. (1990) *Clergy Under Stress*. London: Mowbray.

Foskett, J. (1984) *Meaning in Madness: The Pastor and the Mentally Ill*. London: SPCK.

Foskett, J. (1993) 'Report on recognition and accreditation of Pastoral Work'. *Contact*, 112.

Foskett, J. and Lyall, D. (1988) *Helping the Helpers: Supervision and Pastoral Care*. London: SPCK.

Fowler, J. W. (1981) *Stages of Faith*. New York: Harper & Row.

Fowler, J. W. (1987) *Faith Development and Pastoral Care*. Philadelphia: Fortress.

Frankl, V. (1988) *The Will to Meaning*. New York: Meridian.

Freeman, D. (1988) 'Symbols and Healing: A Personal Perspective of Analysis', *Soul Searching: Studies in Judaism and Psychotherapy*, (ed.) Cooper. London: SCM.

Freud, S. (1905) *Three Essays on the Theory of Sexuality*. London: Penguin Freud Library Volume 5.

Freud, S. (1927a) *The Future of an Illusion*. London: Penguin Freud Library Volume 12.

Freud, S. (1927b) *Postscript to 'The Question of Lay Analysis'*. London: Penguin Freud Library Volume 15.

Freud, S. and Pfister, O. (1963) *Psychoanalysis and Faith*. London: Hogarth Press.

Fromm, E. (1950) *Psychoanalysis and Religion*. New Haven: Yale.

Gaffney, P. D. (1990) 'Islamic Care and Counseling', *Dictionary of Pastoral Care and Counseling*. Nashville: Abingdon.

Gallup, P. J. (1992) '"Subham", The Concept of Wholeness in Pastoral Counseling in the Hindu Cultural Context', *Pastoral Care & Context*. Amsterdam: VU University Press.

Gerkin, C. V. (1984) *The Living Human Document: Re-Visioning Pastoral Counseling in a Hermeneutic Mode*. Nashville: Abingdon.

Gillon, R. (1985) *Philosophical Medical Ethics*. Chichester: Wiley.

Greenberg, J. R. and Mitchell, S. A. (1983) *Object Relations in Psychoanalytic Theory*. Cambridge, Mass: Harvard University Press.

Grollman, E. A. (1990) 'Jewish Care and Counseling', *Dictionary of Pastoral Care and Counseling*. Nashville: Abingdon.

Guntrip, H. (1956) *Mental Pain and the Cure of Souls*. London: Independent Press.

Guntrip, H. (1971) *Psychology for Ministers and Social Workers* (3rd edn). London: George Allen and Unwin.

Hall, C. E. (1992) *Head and Heart: The Story of the Clinical Pastoral Education Movement*. Atlanta: Journal of Pastoral Care Publications.

Halmos, P. (1965) *The Faith of the Counsellors*. London: Constable.

Hay, D. (1987) *Exploring Inner Space* (2nd edn). Oxford: Mowbray.

Hiltner, S. (1949) *Pastoral Counseling*. Nashville: Abingdon.

Hinkle, J. E. (1977) 'The "Robin Hood" Policy: Ethical and Practical Issues Growing Out of the Use of Fee Scales in Pastoral Counseling Centers', *Journal of Pastoral Care*, XXXI, June.

Holifield, E. B. (1983) *A History of Pastoral Care In America*. Nashville: Abingdon.

Hughes, Selwyn (1981) *A Friend in Need*. London: Kingsway.

Hurding, R. F. (1985) *Roots and Shoots: A Guide to Counselling and Psychotherapy*. London: Hodder and Stoughton.

Hurding, R. F. (1992) *The Bible and Counselling*. London: Hodder and Stoughton.

Irvine, A. (1989) 'Isolation in the Parish: The Concept', *Contact*, 98.

Jewett, J. and Haight, E. (1983) 'The Emergence of Feminine Consciousness in Supervision', *The Journal of Supervision and Training in Ministry*, Volume 6. Chicago.

Jacobs, M. (1988) *Towards the Fullness of Christ*. London: Darton, Longman and Todd.

Jacobs, M. (1993a) *Living Illusions*. London: SPCK.

Jacobs, M. (1993b) *A Brief History of the Bi-ennial Consultation at Launde Abbey*. Leicester: University of Leicester Department of Adult Education.

Jones, E. (1964) *The Life and Work of Sigmund Freud*. Harmondsworth: Penguin (abridged edn).

Jung, C. G. (1933) *Modern Man in Search of a Soul*. New York: Harvest.

Kadushin, A. (1985) *Supervision in Social Work*. New York: Columbia.

Katz, R. L. (1985) *Pastoral Care and the Jewish Tradition*. Philadelphia: Fortress.

Katz, R. L. (1987) 'Pastoral Care in Judaism', *Dictionary of Pastoral Care*. London: SPCK.

Kelber, W. (1983) *The Oral and Written Gospel*. Philadelphia: Fortress.

Kelsey, M. (1982) *Christo-Psychology*. London: Darton, Longman and Todd.

Khan, Hazrat Inayat (1989) *Spiritual Dimensions of Psychology*. New Lebanon: Omega.

Khan, Pir Vilayat Inayat (1993) *Counselling and Therapy: The Spiritual Dimension*. New Lebanon: Omega.

Klink, T. (1966) 'Supervision', *Education for Ministry*, (ed.) Fielding. Dayton: American Association of Theological Schools.

Kohlberg, L. (1976) *Collected Papers on Moral Development*. San Francisco: Harpers.

Krebs, R. L. (1980) 'Why Pastors should not be Counselors', *Journal of Pastoral Care*, XXXIV, 4, December.

Kubler-Ross, E. (1969) *On Death and Dying*. London: Tavistock.

Lake, F. (1966) *Clinical Theology*. London: Darton, Longman and Todd (abridged edn by Martin Yeomans, 1986, DLT).

Lake, F. (1981) *Tight Corners in Pastoral Counselling*. London: Darton, Longman and Todd.

Lambourne, R. A. (1970) 'With Love to the USA', *Religion and Medicine*. London: SCM.

Lambourne, R. A. (1971) 'Objections to a National Pastoral Organisation', *Contact*, 35.

Lambourne, R. A. (1974) 'Personal Reformation and Political Formation in Pastoral Care', *Contact*, 44 (also printed in *Journal of Pastoral Care*, XXV, 3, September 1971).

Lasch, C. (1979) *The Culture of Narcissism*. New York: Warner Books.

Lasch, C. (1984) *The Minimal Self: Psychic Survival in Troubled Times*. New York: Norton.

Lee, R. S. (1968) *Principles of Pastoral Counselling*. London: SPCK.

Leech, K. (1977) *Soul Friend*. London: Sheldon.

Leech, K. (1986) *Spirituality and Pastoral Care*. London: SPCK.

Leishman, R. L. and Ritson, B. (1975) 'Working Together in Mental Health', *Contact*, 50.

Lyall, D. (1993) 'Edinburgh 79 – Thirteen Years On', *The Risks of Freedom*, (ed.) Becher *et al.* Manila: Pastoral Care Foundation.

McKenzie, J. G. (1928) *Souls in the Making: An Introduction to Pastoral Psychology*. London: George Allen and Unwin.

McKenzie, J. A. and Moore, R. L. (1983) 'Gender Issues in Supervision', *Journal of Supervision and Training in Ministry*, 6.

McNeill, J. T. (1951) *A History of the Cure of Souls*. New York: Harper and Row.

Martin, Tony (1985) 'Buddhism and Counselling', *Contact*, 87.

Martin, Ted (1986) 'On Feeling Abandoned', *Contact*, 90.

May, G. G. (1992) *Care of Mind: Care of Spirit*. San Francisco: Harper.

Melinsky, H. (1970) 'Clinical Theology: A Survey', *Religion and Medicine*. London: SCM.

Menninger, K. (1958) *Theory of Psychoanalytic Technique*. New York: Basic Books.

Menninger, K. (1973) *Whatever Became of Sin?* New York: Hawthorn.

Merton, T. (1948) *The Seven Storey Mountain*. London: Sheldon.

Merton, T. (1968) *Conjectures of a Guilty Bystander*. New York: Doubleday.

Methodist Church in Britain (1991) *Some Elements of Pastoral Practice: A Discussion Document*, London.

Mills, L. O. (1990) 'Hasidic Care and Counseling', *Dictionary of Pastoral Care and Counseling*. Nashville: Abingdon.

Mowrer, O. Hobart (1961) *The Crisis in Psychiatry and Religion*. Princeton: Van Nostrand.

Mumford, D. (1987) 'May I see a *Christian* Psychiatrist?', *Contact*, 93.

Murphy, J. M. (1990) 'Professionalism', *Dictionary of Pastoral Care and Counseling*. Nashville: Abingdon.

Narramore, S. B. (1990) 'Christian Psychotherapist', *Dictionary of Pastoral Care and Counseling*. Nashville: Abingdon.

Northcott, M. S. (1990) 'The Case Study Method', *Contact*, 103.

Northcott, M. S. (1992) *The New Age and Pastoral Theology: Towards the Resurgence of the Sacred*. Edinburgh: Contact Pastoral Monograph, 2.

Oates, W. E. (1962) *Protestant Pastoral Counseling*. Philadelphia: Westminster.

Oates, W. E. (1974) *Pastoral Counseling*. Philadelphia: Westminster.

Oden, T. C. (1966) *Kerygma and Counseling*. Philadelphia: Westminster.

Oden, T. C. (1984) *Care of Souls in the Classical Tradition*. Philadelphia: Fortress.

Oden, T. C. (1989) *Pastoral Counsel*. New York: Crossroad.

Oswald, R. M. and Kroeger, O. (1988) *Personality Type and Religious Leadership*. Washington: Alban Institute.

Pattison, M. E. (1972) 'Systems Pastoral Care', *Journal of Pastoral Care*, XXVI, 1, March.

Patton, J. (1983) *Pastoral Counseling: A Ministry of the Church*. Nashville: Abingdon.

Patton, J. (1990) 'Personal Story, Symbol and Myth in Pastoral Care', *Dictionary of Pastoral Care and Counseling*. Nashville: Abingdon.

Patton, J. (1993) *Pastoral Care in Context*. Louisville: Westminster/John Knox.

Peck, M. S. (1987) *The Different Drum*. London: Arrow Books.

Perry, J. (1993) *Counselling for Women*. Buckingham: Open University Press.

Piaget, J. (1950) *The Psychology of Intelligence*. London: Routledge and Kegan Paul.

Powell, R. C. (1975) *CPE: Fifty Years of Learning Through Supervised Encounter With Living Human Documents*. New York: The Association for Clinical Pastoral Education.

Ramon, Brother (1989) *Soul Friends*. London: Marshall Pickering.

Rassieur, C. L. (1976) *The Problem Clergymen Don't Talk About*. Philadelphia: Westminster.

Rice, H. L. (1991) *Reformed Spirituality*. Louisville: Westminster/John Knox.

Rogers, C. R. (1942) *Counseling and Psychotherapy*. Boston: Houghton Mifflin.

Rogers, C. R. (1951) *Client-Centered Therapy*. Boston: Houghton Mifflin.

Rogers, C. R. (1961) *On Becoming a Person*. Boston: Houghton Mifflin.

Rogers, C. R. (1980) *A Way of Being*. Boston: Houghton Mifflin.

Rokeach, M. (1960) *The Open and Closed Mind*. New York: Basic Books.

Ross, R. J. (1990) 'Fees in Pastoral Counseling', *Dictionary of Pastoral Care and Counseling*. Nashville: Abingdon.

Rothwell, N. (1993) 'Natural Healing', *Clinical Psychology Forum*, 55.

Rutter, P. (1989) *Sex in the Forbidden Zone*. New York: Ballantine.

Rycroft, C. (1972) 'Reparation', *A Critical Dictionary of Psychoanalysis*. London: Penguin.

Scharfenberg, J. (1987) *Pastoral Care as Dialogue*. Philadelphia: Fortress.

Selby, P. (1983) *Liberating God: Private Care and Public Struggle*. London: SPCK.

Shaw, D. W. D. (1978) *The Dissuaders*. London: SCM.

Soddy, K. (1964) 'Institute of Religion and Medicine', *Contact*, 11.

Speck, P. (1988) *Being There: Pastoral Care in Times of Illness*. London: SPCK.

Stein, E. V. (1968) *Guilt: Theory and Therapy*. Philadelphia: Westminster.

Stein. E. V. (1990) 'Guilt', *Dictionary of Pastoral Care and Counseling*. Nashville: Abingdon.

Sunderland, R. H. (1988) 'Lay Pastoral Care', *Journal of Pastoral Care*, XLII, 2, Summer.

Switzer, D. (1983) 'Why Pastors *Should* be Counselors (of a Sort)', *Journal of Pastoral Care*, XXVII, 1, March.

Thorne, B. (1991) *Person-Centred Counselling*. London: Whurr.

Thornton. E. E. (1970) *Professional Education for Ministry*. Nashville: Abingdon.

Thornton, E. E. (1979) 'The Risks of Freedom', *Journal of Pastoral Care*, XXXIII, 3, 146.

Thornton, M. (1956) *Pastoral Theology: A Reorientation*. London: SPCK.

Thornton, M. (1984) *Spiritual Direction*. London: SPCK.

Thornton, M. (1990) 'Spiritual Direction, History and Traditions of', *Dictionary of Pastoral Care and Counseling*. Nashville: Abingdon.

Thurneysen, E. (1962) *A Theology of Pastoral Care*. Richmond: John Knox Press.

Tillich, P. (1949) 'You Are Accepted', *The Shaking of the Foundations*. London: SCM.

Tillich, P. (1952) *The Courage to Be*. London: Fontana.

Tillich, P. (1959) 'The Theology of Pastoral Care', *Pastoral Psychology*, October, 21–6.

Tracy, D. (1983) 'The Foundations of Practical Theology', in D. S. Browning (ed.) *Practical Theology*. San Francisco: Harper and Row.

Truax, C. B. and Carkuff, R. R. (1967) *Toward Effective Counseling and Psychotherapy*. Chicago: Aldine.

Tyndall, N. (1993) *Counselling in the Voluntary Sector*. Buckingham: Open University Press.

Tyrell, B. J. (1982) *Christotherapy II*. New York: Paulist.

Walters, L. (1986) 'Confidentiality', *New Dictionary of Christian Ethics*. London: SCM.

Weatherhead, L. D. (1951) *Psychology, Religion and Healing*. London: Hodder and Stoughton.

Weatherly, M. (1993) 'National Vocational Qualifications', Oxford: Clinical Theology Association.

Wharton, M. (1983) 'Pastoral Studies in an Anglican Theological College', *Contact*, 78.

Wilkinson, A. B. (1986) *The Scottish Law of Evidence*. London: Butterworth.

Winton, M. and Cameron, J. (1986) 'Stress and Burnout in the Ministry', *Contact*, 90.

Wise, C. (1951) *Pastoral Counseling*. New York: Harper.

Wise, C. (1980) *Pastoral Psychotherapy*. New York: Jason Aronson.

Wray, I. (1986) 'Buddhism and Psychotherapy', in G. Claxton (ed.) *Beyond Therapy*. London: Wisdom Publications.

Wright, D. (1970) 'On Looking Into Yourself', *The Listener*, 84, 2172.

Young, M. C. (1989) 'Professional and Ethical Issues for Ministers Who Counsel', *Journal of Pastoral Care*, XLIII, 3, Fall.

Index

COUNSELLING FOR WOMEN
Janet Perry

Although few in number, organizations which provide counselling services for women have had a tremendous impact on our current understanding of women's psychology and the issues women explore in counselling. Through her examination of these organizations, Janet Perry highlights the unique emphasis they place on the importance of how services are provided and their exploration of the dynamics of the working relationships of women counsellors. The organizations included in the book range from Women's Aid to Women's Therapy Centres and their services are considered in the context of counselling women. The study shows that through a self-reflexive examination of their organizational processes, these agencies have come to a greater understanding of the ways in which women working with women create non-hierarchical and cooperative endeavours, much needed in our individualistic and competitive society. The book illustrates the conflicts that arise when both modes seek to exist within one organization – Family Service Units – and the struggle all the agencies have to legitimize these ways of working to a male dominated system from which funding is often sought. Recommended reading for all those involved in counselling and psychotherapy, this book illustrates some of the practical outcomes of these alternative working models.

Contents
The development of counselling in women's organizations – Counselling in women's organizations – The practice of counselling women – Specific issues in counselling women – Professional relationships in counselling for women – Critique of counselling for women – References – Index.

128pp   0 335 19034 0 (Paperback)

COUNSELLING IN INDEPENDENT PRACTICE
Gabrielle Syme

This book demonstrates and reflects the care and responsibility that must be taken by anyone considering counselling in independent practice. It is a thoughtful book based upon the experience of a skilled and well-trained practitioner who has set her own standards high. For anyone contemplating setting up in private or independent practice as a counsellor or psychotherapist it offers an excellent model. It explores in depth the practical, ethical and personal issues that should be considered before taking such a major step. Concluding with a critique of private and independent practice, the book makes a powerful contribution to the current debate about the difference between the minimum standards set by Codes of Ethics and Practice for counsellors and what is good practice. The professional practitioner will recognize the points of discussion raised by the author. For this group, the book provides a yardstick by which to assess the quality of service they provide and the relationship that they maintain with their clients. With its useful exploration of this relationship, the book will also be of interest to anyone considering counselling or psychotherapeutic help, and those referring patients or colleagues.

Contents

The development of counselling in independent practice – Counselling in independent practice – The practice of counselling in independent practice – Specific issues in counselling in independent practice – Professional relationships in counselling in independent practice – A critique of counselling in independent practice – Appendices – References – Index.

160pp   0 335 19049 9 (Paperback)

COUNSELLING IN THE VOLUNTARY SECTOR
Nicholas Tyndall

Nicholas Tyndall has drawn upon his extensive experience of counselling and training in personal and family organizations to provide a comprehensive picture of the voluntary sector. In his clear, accessible style, he outlines the beginnings of counselling in Britain and charts the development of the growing number of specialist and generic agencies.

The book is written in the firm belief that the voluntary sector can combine what is best in the amateur and the professional. Its scope and practices are explored. Methods of selection, training and supervision of counsellors are compared, and the challenges facing staff and management committees are examined. The book highlights the strengths and weaknesses of voluntary counselling, and identifies the need to improve equal opportunities, fill new gaps and develop inter-agency collaboration. The author has harsh words for public bodies which have high expectations of volunteers but are not prepared to meet the cost. He offers helpful advice for existing agencies and those wanting to improve their personal services; and guidance to individuals who are interested in becoming counsellors.

Contents
The development of counselling in the voluntary sector – Voluntary agencies – The practice of counselling in the voluntary sector – Specific issues in counselling in the voluntary sector – Professional relationships in counselling in the voluntary sector – A critique of counselling in the voluntary sector – References – Index.

160pp   0 335 19027 8 (Paperback)